CW00519337

# Contents

# One: Your Mind is a Liar

Your Mind is a consummate liar. Why on earth, you may ask, is this **good** news? Well, if you are listening to this book because of the title then you probably suspect (or more bluntly <u>**know**</u>) that there are some things about yourself that you wish you didn't believe. But you do.

You probably also '<u>**know**</u>' that you can't change. You certainly wouldn't admit it to anyone but maybe... just maybe... you're a bit - or a lot -desperate. Perhaps you've spent a lot of money on e-books and courses and maybe even taken some personal development trainings. But what you read or visualise or listen to or chant or tap - doesn't stick.

And so - deep down - you think that the bad things you think about yourself are *true*. It may only be a suspicion or perhaps you are full-blown hiding from that deep knowing that you *are* bad, stupid, unwanted etc.

I was there for *over twenty years*. I was that person who, beneath it all, felt unwanted and like there was no place for me in the world. I resisted the idea that I was unchangeable but deep down I also sort of 'knew' I could not do it. I could not change.

For over 20 years I studied Neuro Linguistic Programming (NLP) and Neurosemantics up to Trainer level, learned EFT, Emotrance, 2x2, Be Set Free Fast (BSFF), Future-visioning - and so many other things I feel I have forgotten as much as I have learned! I made some shifts in beliefs about myself, some by accident more than design. But the core beliefs mostly remained.

I *was* (and am) loved (I have an amazing wife), have six children (biological and step children) good friends, and many achievements. I have been a Christian for 19 years and that definitely **has** saved my life. But when that desperation and hurt came, sometimes even that did not seem to be enough.

So what changed? Two things happened: I finally realised why most attempts to change fail AND I started to take seriously something I first read about 23 years ago. Together, they gave me hope and confidence that I could change.

The first answer I already gave you but you probably passed over it without understanding how significant it is.

# FOREWORD

"Nobody begins self-study as an "A" student. In fact, real self-study begins with becoming aware of just how unaware we really are. Don't let this last thought throw you! It's wise to see where our wisdom was only an assumption. This allows real wisdom, real self-knowledge, to grow. And this explains why some of our most important first lessons come when we set an exercise for ourselves, and later see that we altogether forgot about it…. Beginning to see that we're lost in thought all day is a valuable signal to us. It's equivalent to the doctor's diagnosis that is the necessary first step towards achieving a cure.

We should never be discouraged by any discovery our self-study shows us. To be aware that we have been unaware is the beginning of real awareness…there can never be failure, but only new opportunities for growth."

*Guy Finlay: The Intimate Enemy: Winning the War Within Yourself*

**You don't change because you secretly think the things you believe about yourself are TRUE!**

Think about it. If these 'bad' things about you are TRUE then you can't change them because you can't change TRUTH, right? That is the mind's psycho-logical attitude and is not the same logic as regular logic. With psycho-logic a glance can 'mean' she hates me or a feather can become an object of fear. Not logical, right? Psycho-logical.

In order for you to truly start changing what needs to happen? You need to come to deeply **KNOW** that while your mind can to be trusted to do many things, in many ways it is extremely unreliable as a source of 'ultimate Truth'. It will do everything it can to convince you YOUR perceptions are right and everyone else is wrong. And because its bias is 'you are always right' that makes it wise to be learn some of its tricks and have a healthy dose of 'thank you mind - but let's check anyway'!

Your mind - like people - has strange quirks which you need to get used to and work with… but let's start easily with an example using people.

I once worked with a man who used to get agitated if he had to deal with too many difficult enquiries in a row at the customer serving counter. He was a generous and hard worker in many other regards yet when I saw his face start to get flushed and his eyes darting about I used to send him out to the back office to do some work there until he calmed down.

I didn't have to tell him why but we both understood it was best because we both knew what he was like. If I left him on the counter, he could actually end up being rude to customers because he was very stressed.

So, because I understood how he operated, – that at certain times I had to change the way I managed him to still get the best out of him – I was able to retain smooth functioning of the staff counter.

Your mind has certain quirks that you need to understand – for example – the mind tends to ignore evidence that does not agree with its conclusions. Knowing this means you can ask yourself if you are ignoring something *even* if you feel <u>certain</u> you are not - simply because you also know your mind lies to you.

You need to learn some of the ways YOU operate (and lie to yourself) and adjust your thinking accordingly to compensate for this.

Once you understand – and ACCEPT – how your mind operates – no matter how dark your mood - you can force yourself to ask: 'What could I be missing?' What am I assuming? If I were compensating for my inbuilt biases what additional questions would I ask myself?

Of course, if you want to continue being driven by your moods and don't want to be a better thinker then just carry on the way you are. It's your choice.

**The main purpose of this book is to help give you a shift in philosophy about the 'Truthfulness' of your thoughts.**

No, not empty vacuous arguments that you'll forget about after listening... deep shifts in your points of view which will help you shift your beliefs which, after all, help run your life.

Throughout this book I'm going to give you some brief exercises to do. These are intended to give your mind the experience that *change **is** possible*. They may be the key you need although my overall intention is to encourage you to study fuller versions of the material which I will point to.

I know it may be disappointing that I am not promising guaranteed change but if you strongly consider (on multiple occasions) whether what I am writing to you is credible there *will* be some changes in your philosophy – or at least enough to give you the hope that change is really possible and help give you the impetus to go and work on it.

I know some of you will sigh that there is yet more work to do after reading this: I felt that way twenty years ago (I've been working on myself for 23 years) BUT you have the benefit of my experience which can help you shorten the process. If I were to write a book that covered all the methods, I have used it would probably be over 1000 pages long and break a lot of copyright laws. Plus, I am not an expert on every change method although I have used many for as much time as I felt them useful.

So I will call it 'further study' and tell you WHY I think you should investigate. Then, it is up to you.

I've marked some of these sections STOP AND THINK and it is to your benefit to find somewhere quiet to do them. Studies have shown that even the ringing of a telephone in the background affects concentration. I bought some industrial workman's ear muffs off Amazon for £7.00 to block out all sound!

## STOP AND THINK

**A quick note on repetition!**

Many self-help books are bought like lunchtime sandwiches: to be read/eaten once and never returned too. If you truly want the freedom of mastering your lying mind this will not do.

You will find I repeat myself a few times in this book. I am not ashamed of that. I learned over the years that 'repetition is the mother of integration' simply meaning that I realise, just at TV advertisers do, that repeat viewings and hearing aid the acceptance of a particular point of view. So yes, I repeat myself. Yes, it is for you own good.

You trained yourself into bad thinking habits (through repetition) and now you have to train yourself out of them. One read of this book may shift some perspectives but some exercises you will have to do until they are second nature.

For example, practicing silence – one of the exercises to come - and stepping back from what you think and evaluating your thoughts **is something you will need to do for the rest of your lif**e because you - and the world - are always changing.

You may have to be quite aggressive and persistent in questioning yourself at times: at other times you can ask the question and sleep on it - or do something else until an answer comes. But I assure you unless you take on board some or most of these ideas you will not change. They need to become tools in your armory.

I don't mind if you test them with a healthy suspicion – you can always stop or discard using them – but keep on until you get results. Yes, you are acting on faith but when are you not? I recently read that human excrement has been found in with the ice put in fizzy drinks at KFC – but I drank the drinks on faith that they were healthy – until now! You may not be 'religious' but your whole life from crossing the road to eating KFC(!) is an exercise in faith!

**A note on contradicting myself and context**

If you're older than 10 you've probably started to figure out that the world is contradictory at times!  For example, unless you're the child of an extremist, your parents will probably tell you it's 'bad to hate'. Yet, it's not bad to 'hate' poverty if that feeling motivates you to get wealthy. Or you could 'hate' injustice if it helps you change the world for the better. Then again, to 'hate' injustice too much can lead to being over-rigorous in the application of the rules and sometimes people need a little grace and forgiveness to help them change.

When I was 19 I faked a date on a train ticket and the transport police caught me.

I deserved to be fined and get a criminal record. But I told them I was going to college and if my parents had to pay this fine I could not go. They were gracious, gave me a warning, and I went off relived and determined not to break the law again!

Context is important. So when I tell you in this book that you need to eliminate 'doubt' and yet mention using doubt as a tool I will talking about it *in different contexts*.

For example, in order to manifest something you desire your focus needs to be pure and without doubt but if you have limiting beliefs then doubt is a powerful tool to use *on purpose* to eliminate those beliefs.

Someone once said that genius was the ability to hold two opposing ideas in mind at once. You *can* do this and your thinking will be healthier for it. 'Thinking is hard work', said Henry Ford 'which is why so many men don't do it.' But like a muscle – work it baby – and you'll get stronger.

When I was 19 and about to start college I tried to visualize. For the first three days I could barely see anything in my mind's eye except smudges of colour and flashes of light. But I kept at it and as a result of my practice I was able to learn memory systems to memorize multiple dates. Right now I can easily imagine myself walking the streets of my favorite city in South America. Work your mind like a muscle and it will get stronger.

---

# Two: The Starting Point: Getting Control of Your Mind

To repeat: The reason treating your brain as a *liar* is so essential is that **it is designed to treat everything you think AS TRUTH**. Along with the good, healthy positive thoughts, that includes all the awful, toxic, self-hating and inaccurate beliefs about yourself and the world. And <u>every</u> thought you have either helps you or harms you – no matter whether you are aware of it or not.

How could it not? Scientists think every part of your brain is linked to every other. Those thoughts are not like some unused part of computer memory waiting to be accessed – I think those parts are always being accessed and contribute to your overall outlook on life.

## STOP AND THINK

Try a little thought experiment: if every part of you supported you to achieve the best possible life for you – how would that feel?

Hold on that feeling for a moment – and then compare it to how you feel usually. My guess is you realise there is a difference – and that is good – you realise there is some work still to be done.

If you were to see a cognitive therapist he or she would work to help you adjust your thoughts and beliefs to 'healthy' ones that would enable you to operate 'normally' in society. I'm highlighting these terms because 'healthy' and normal are going, to some extent, going to differ depending on where you are in the world.

(Of course, I trust beliefs like 'murder is bad' are ones you consider healthy wherever you are!)

Once you are back in control of your mind – and regularly evaluating and changing your thoughts - *You* are going to have to decide what counts as 'normal' and 'healthy'. That's a heavy responsibility and probably a reason why so many people turn to religion and philosophy for answers. Plus, who wants to be normal anyway? If you're going to be truly successful, you can't think like 'normal people'!

I equally suggest that the lack of a coherent code for living – one that is consciously thought out and being lived and tested for its healthiness – is the reason that so many people are nihilistic and hedonistic... in other words, cynical and depressed – and addicted to pleasures. The Bible says 'without vision, the people perish' and human beings are naturally teleological – we will strive to achieve goals whether healthy for us or not.

I have, over the years, found answers I am satisfied with and I am still exploring. If you want to hear my conclusions, they are in the last chapter.

However, before you develop that code or consider adding new philosophies to your life you first need to get control of your mind.

I know you might be eager just to jump in and just learn new ideas but trust me, without some mastering of these your task will be much more difficult. Your mind *belongs to you* although if you cannot do these exercises at will, it almost certainly needs reminding who is in charge! Let's start with the most important ability: silencing your mind.

**Silence is golden**

It may seem odd to start a chapter on silence talking about money but when a multi-millionaire (and other wealthy people who use his work) say that stilling their minds form the base foundation of their success, it's worth listening.

Andy Shaw, multi-millionaire creator of the Bug Free Mind system, points out again and again in his books and talks that if you cannot still your mind; how can you focus on creating what you desire?

Backing up from that – if you cannot stop your racing thoughts and rapid shifts in focus – from THIS thought – to THAT thought – to THOSE thoughts - how are going to concentrate long enough to change those thoughts? This is where you need to start.

You need a way to slow your thoughts down so you can observe and evaluate them. How can you judge the lies if you cannot catch them in the act! Plus, as an added bonus: knowing you can create peace of mind at a moment's notice gives you a powerful confidence in handling yourself! I simply cannot explain the confidence that comes from knowing you can get your mind to SHUT UP and also to direct it at will to your purposes. It's like taming a wild stallion – all that power now at your command.

In my other book *The Millionaire Silence* I talk about how to use the following technique to generate solutions and ways of making money but the basic technique is extremely powerful by itself and an essential bedrock for what follows:

## Silencing your Mind

The challenge is this: to make your mind devoid of thoughts for 15 seconds. Yep, only 15 seconds. Should be easy, right?

To be clear that is 15 seconds where you do not let your mind wander: you do not talk to yourself in your mind nor hear sounds/conversation from memories or imaginings. You do not see pictures nor mental movies. You do not smell or taste anything with your mind. You observe (if you have your eyes open) but with no commentary of any kind.

Nothing. Nada. You can hear your breathing, and maybe other sounds if your location is not quiet. But you don't let those sounds draw your attention or make judgements about them. If you do – you start again.

I use an online stopwatch to help me : just search on Google and one will come up.

You can also download apps from your phone's app store. It helps to have the timer running so you don't start wondering if your 15 seconds are up.

It is unlikely that you'll manage the 15 seconds the first time.

It took me weeks to get up to that and now I can manage around 48 seconds up to about a minute-and-a-half.

Just practice a few times a day and don't be too hard on yourself. Before long you'll find yourself able to still your mind more and more effectively. There are considerable medical benefits to being able to do this as well.

This is not meditation or mindfulness**. You are not concentrating on sounds or candles or watching your thoughts. That's something else.

If you are doing this properly at some point you'll feel your mental and physical state shift into a kind of calm where you are still yet moving and clear headed yet absent of the rush of thoughts you may usually have.

You can just sit and enjoy this and when you are ready, use the next skill.

**There are no religious connotations to doing this. It is simply helping your mind work more effectively: by slowing down your thoughts you can actually think faster! However, if you do pray it can really help to still your mind before you commune with God.

# Three: The Step Back Skill

In the last chapter I mentioned observing. Would you like to understand what you are doing when you 'observe' and why you never have to be truly mentally 'stuck'?

It's because you, unlike any other creature on the planet, *can always think about your thoughts*. You can think about your LAST thought – the one you just had; or any other thought you can bring to mind. If you asked yourself: Can I? or even said: 'No, I can't!' then you just did!

Michael Hall, Ph.d. and creator of the field of Neurosemantics, calls this 'the step back skill' because by consciously using it you can 'step back', and mentally 'create a space' whereby you can:

- Think ABOUT it
- Reflect ON it
- Rise ABOVE IT
- Chew OVER it

Do you see what's going on here? Even our language supports this idea that when we want to evaluate an idea we mentally 'rise above it' so that we now have a space for thinking and the thought we are thinking about. So we actually 'step back' to get some distance – but that distance is also a step up above it to 'get some perspective'.

Why all this technical talk? Because once you are more able to still your mind you will have easier access to becoming aware of the thoughts and beliefs in it.

## STOP AND THINK

Try it now. Take a moment to calm your mind and observe your thinking like someone watching clouds scud across the sky:

You can then ask yourself questions like:

- What do I believe about myself?
- What do I believe about my place in the world?
- Am I important? Significant?
- What don't I like about myself?
- What do I like about myself?

When the answers come you can hold them in mind – because your mind is still – and then STEP back and ask yourself of the answers:

- Is this true?
- Is this really true?
- Is this healthy for me?
- Is this thought useful in helping me where I want to go?
- Do I still want it?
- Who would I be without these thoughts/beliefs?
- Would I sell this thought to my children?
- If I don't want this thought, how much do I not want it?
- What would I like to think instead?

Doing this can weaken or even change those thoughts. I cannot promise it will definitely work straight away for you because the human mind is complex and belief change can be more complex than just deciding you don't want to think something. (It doesn't have to be, by the way, it just sometimes is.)

But it can work and sometimes just hearing yourself say that you believe something is REALLY stupid is enough to change it.

Practice during the day: set your watch/smartphone timer – on vibrate if at work – and when it goes off ask yourself: What am I thinking about right now? And what do I think about that? The first question gets you to step back/up from your current thoughts in mind: the second starts to reveal what the thoughts are about your thoughts.

The reason doing this is so important is that until we are aware of what is in our minds we cannot evaluate or change it.

**How powerful is observation…really?**

Physicists tell us that merely watching an experiment changes the way the items in it behave. I'm not sure what their explanation is for why this happens but there is a way to demonstrate the power of the mind to affect things by paying attention to them.

I know you won't believe me when I tell you but simply by directing concentrated attention at a fluffy cloud in the sky you can cause it to dissolve. It's called cloud bursting and I've been doing it for about ten years.

The first time I heard about it was from a guy called Neil Slade www.neilslade.com who says he heard about it from Art Bell in the seventies and *he* said his grandfather was doing it in the 1930's.

You can find instructions at that website but to do it, you need to visualize your amygdale first. Put each thumb at the corner of your eye on either side of your nose. Let the first finger of each hand fall onto each side of your head, on your temple. The amygdale are an almond shaped organ and there is one about an inch under each first finger.

Now, imagine that each one has a little light switch in it. Imagine that light switch flipping down to the on position. You have just 'clicked your amygdale'. You may feel a burst of energy or a full blown pleasure explosion. Or you may feel nothing, the first time is different for everyone.

Now, find a find a fluffy cloud (summertime is obviously best) and imagine beams of energy streaming from your amygdale until you start seeing a hole or holes appear in the cloud. Keep it up and usually within a few minutes the cloud is gone.

The first time I did it I was utterly shocked. I tested the process again, and again. I rang a friend. She tested it and called me back excitedly – she had done it too.

Why this talk of dissolving clouds? Well, putting the incredible implications of this aside for now, if you can affect the local weather system of planet earth by paying concentrated attention to a cloud then it's plausible that your thoughts can be influenced and change just by observing and paying attention to them.

My understanding is that, as you observe your thoughts from 'the position of power' – a higher meta position - you are layering feelings of acceptance and non-judgement onto them – which tends to change them to something less 'hot' to experience. It's like a cool hand on a fevered brow. Amazing stuff – and it works.

### Slapping down a TPIC

Practitioners of the mind-changing set of processes called Neuro-Linguistic Programming refer to two ways of experiencing an emotional state: associated and dissociated.

'Dissociated' refers to when you are mentally watching yourself – for example, seeing yourself riding a roller-coaster.

'Associated' refers to experiencing the emotional state from the inside of your body – imagine riding the roller coaster right now with your knuckles turning white as you plunge down the next slope.

ARGHHHHHHHHHHHHHHHHHHHHHHHHHHHHHHHHHHHHHHHHHHHHHH HHHHHHHHHHHHHHHHHHHHHHHHHHH!

That's being associated. And being 'associated' into your anger – experiencing it fully and completely from the inside usually leads to a loss of consciousness. No, you are not knocked out. Rather you are not aware that there is any other way of thinking or behaving in that moment.

So, how does that relate to a TIPC? And what the heck is it?

It's what Guy Finlay calls a 'Temporary Person In Control' and it's a fun way to refer to and work with emotional states that try to take you over.

Don't pretend you don't know what I mean! One moment you're fine and then you see someone giving you THAT look and immediately you've been hijacked! You feel ticked off or sexy or thoughtful or something completely different to the way you just felt.

If it's a strong feeling then you'll feel like it's the TRUTH and you've always felt this way.

As an example, some years ago I went to the New Forest in the UK with my wife who is black. When we went downstairs to breakfast EVERYONE was white except her. And I really felt like they were looking at us and judging us.

So I glared at the whole room and loudly exclaimed: 'Yes, she's with me!' I was indignant, self righteous, and I'd let myself get hijacked by a mindset that said ;'You're a bunch of racists!'

Were they? Who knows – and who cares! But at the time I was not self-aware enough to feel the emotional state coming on and stop it.

Now, I say 'Oh hi, TPIC!' how are you doing? You want to take me over? You're not real you know although if I give in I know you'll feel real. Just pass by buddy, just pass by!'

A TPIC makes you feel like you have an identity as a *wronged* person, a *sexy* person etc. It feels good to know *who you are*, doesn't it?

Only this emotional state is NOT who you are! It's like a brain parasite that makes you think everything is normal. I recently saw a documentary about a parasite on a caterpillar that actually makes it wriggle out into full view of birds so it can be eaten! It's called a Zombie bug or something like that.

Your TPIC when unchallenged makes you into a zombie – and when you wake up – you think: 'Wow, that behavior was not like me at-all'. You got possessed buddy!

So in the interests of staying in control and directing your life as you consciously want to – start to observe your thoughts and when you feel a strong emotion coming on – step back and say 'hello TPIC!'

It may feel uncomfortable to do so but you remain in the decision position of power. A ounce of pain is worth a ton of regret, believe me!

**A Secret about the step back/up skill and 'stuckness'**

As the song goes: 'I've saved the best till last'. When you are 'thinking something over': maybe making a decision **about** something – does it not feel like your mind is in the position of power?

You may never have thought about it *but actively thinking about your options puts you in the decision-position.* And cognitively 'the thought at the top is in charge of the lot'. Want proof?

Have you ever been angry about something and then a funny thought entered your mind and you collapsed laughing? That funny thought entered your mind as a top thought ABOUT the lower thoughts and its dominant effect cascaded all the way down your thought processes humoring them as it went!

You see, we are never really 'stuck'! If you want to learn more about this 'meta-stating' process you should read either *Meta-States* or *Winning the Inner Game* by Michael Hall – or go to his website and read the beginner articles at www.neurosemantics.com

I studied Meta-States for years and it has given me a calm confidence that I can understand the workings of my mind well enough to direct it. When I remember too...!

Some years ago I spoke to legendary creativity pioneer Win Wenger www.winwenger.com and he told me 'If there's one principle I live by it's this: there's always more.'

Consider that 'being stuck' may simply mean a lack of knowing what the 'more' is – not that there ARE no other options.

When I feel really stuck I remind myself that Einstein taught we could never solve problems at the level they were created. I tell myself: 'I'm still using the old thinking: What would it be like if I were completely starting over with fresh thinking: what would I think? If I had never thought the old thinking what would be the best thoughts I could put in place? What would happen if I went to sleep and a miracle occurred and I woke up the next morning and everything had changed for the better?'

Try it.

lo seem real. By real, I mean they seem like *they* ARE the truth and sometimes it seems like we cannot resist their message; we *have* to do what they say/prompt.

Even worse, when we mentally 'push' against them they just seem to resist and even come back stronger. How wretched we feel! How helpless. Then how angry - and even depressed.

It's so ironic – if I asked you if you knew that other people believed different things; believed *better* things than you, *healthier* things – then you would say 'Yes! Of course I know' and *yet* it might not occur to you that you could *change* your thoughts to be more like theirs. Because, deep down, you still believe your thoughts are genuine simply because they are yours – and you wouldn't lie to yourself, would you?

*In the film, The Matrix, Morpheus says to Neo "Do you want to know WHAT it is?"*

This is the trap… the Matrix of your mind… you are the fish swimming in the water of your mind that you never questioned was there because it is *where you live*…. And it all seems so…well.. natural. Glub.

But it isn't…

In the film (which will help you understand what I am explaining in a more visual and explosive way!) human beings are imprisoned in pods which capture and use the body's electricity. Their brains are wired to the machine and fed stimulus (pictures, sounds and feelings, tastes and smells) that seem so real they over-ride what people would normally experience with their natural senses. They are made to experience a world that seems just like the world in 1999 and *they never question that it might be an illusion because it feels so real.*

Many people got excited about The Matrix because what it portrays is a metaphor for how we personally perceive the world. We think our thoughts (pictures, sounds, feelings we experience and generate ourselves) ARE the Truth so we often don't question them. They key to transformation – and it really is no harder - *and as hard-* as this: to learn to see your mind for what it is – a programmed system of instructions that interact with your organic body and make you see 'reality' a certain way.

We all do see the world different ways – for instance, why do you learn the customs of other nationalities before you visit their country? Is it not because their beliefs are their reality? In Bulgaria, people nod their head for NO and shake it left to right for YES. Those are the meanings they have given to those actions. We don't do that or agree that is what it means. But to them it is just normal. It's their reality and whether you agree with it or not you can respect it.

You must learn to take a step back from the workings of your mind and learn to see it for what it really is…. Code and instructions…which can be changed to create a more effective and happier view of life.

In the written version of this book I show a screenshot of some coding for the ZX Spectrum, an eighties computer. It's full of numbered lines of code and strange terms such as PEEK and POKE and also IF…THEN statements.

For example, if we were talking about the game Space Invaders, then the coding might say: IF players ship is hit by a missile THEN run the routine for an exploding ship.

The point is that the code, the program, instructs the computer what to put on screen, how to respond when you press fire and every other aspect of the behaviour of the game.

*The inner programming determines what is seen on the outer screen.*

Imagine for a moment that you have inner programming which causes you to 'see' (perceive) the world a certain way. Why? Because you do.

An English translation of the Jewish Talmud says: 'We do not see things as they are. We see things as *we* are.'[my emphasis] So *your* thoughts (the program) cause you to perceive the world as YOU think it is which may be accurate or not.

So if you feel threatened by tall people, for instance, your mind will generate feelings of threat whenever you see then REGARDLESS of what they are actually doing! That's the mental routine: IF person over 6ft THEN picture them towering over you about to hurt you.

If you drank too much whisky, threw up and now can't stand the smell that does not make whisky objectively disgusting. It is only disgusting to you. That's your nervous system generating reactions to the world and making you think it's true. And it is 'true' to you. But only to you.

You need to learn to see and re-evaluate the code you program yourself with – and I will teach you some of this – but first you need to believe that the code exists.

You need to acknowledge that your view of the world is not 'just the way it is' but the way you think it is and, if it is not getting you the results you want you can adjust your thinking and your approach instead of just getting vexed that things are not going YOUR way. After all, there are six billion people in the world each with their own 'reality'. Is it really true that they are all wrong and you are right?

Let's look at an example from the Matrix again. I apologise for the spoilers if you haven't seen it yet.

Near the end of the film the hero Neo is confronting enemy agents in a corridor. One shoots him, and instead of dying, he comes back to life because of his belief that He is The One. That belief has over-ruled the normal rules about dying in the Matrix.

He realizes that, as his mind makes the rules about how this world acts, he can break the hold of the Matrix and change the way his world behaves:

Then he begins to see the world as it really is – a set of instructions to his brain that build illusions that seem real. We are treated to a scene of a world made up of streaming lines of computer code which is the programming generating the illusion of the Matrix.

Don't get me wrong. I am not saying we can stop bullets or change the form of buildings by mental power alone – see the film **Inception** for this! But we can change our perceptions of the world and thus become aware of new possibilities for behaving and feeling. We can reprogram and thus alter our own perceptual 'Matrix' and what seemed to be so real in our world dissolves.

Here's putting it a different way.

You may have heard the famous saying: 'The map is not the territory'. I'm going to explain what it means and how it relates to you.

In the print version of the book I showed a map from above of the layout of the world famous St Paul's Cathedral, in London. It's a structural diagram of the walls and it's obviously JUST a map, it's not St Paul's cathedral itself.

Then I showed a photo of the actual St Paul's Cathedral.

I know this seems really obvious to point out but that picture has way more detail than the navigation map above it *but it is still not St Paul's cathedral itself.* It's still actually a map, a guide to what the building looks like in 'objective reality'.

*Both* pictures are maps: visual guides – the first one helps you understand the structure of St Paul's – so it might make it easier to walk around it – and the second gives you more details about its appearance than the first. But never in your right mind would you say that the picture IS St Paul's cathedral.

Maps are supposed to have less detail than the actual experience/location itself – their job is to help you effectively relate to or guide yourself around or through something.

They are not intended to BE THE TRUTH about a thing because they are not that thing. A photo of an apple is NOT the apple itself. The photo is a re-presentation (representation) of the apple. It is technically accurate to point this out to someone who insists a picture of a particular fruit is an apple – but you might just annoy them with your rightness!!

So maps have the following qualities:

If accurate, they have a similar structure to the actual experience. So an accurate road map has lines which should correspond to the actual road layout.

They have deleted lots of information that would be present in the actual experience. The first map does not show the walls of the cathedral are made of stone. The shop of St Paul's cathedral on the map is just a dot.

They contain generalizations: they show all grass as green when it is different shades of green, and yellow in the summer heat.

They distort information – again, the St Paul's shop is represented by a dot but the actual shop obviously doesn't look like this. A dot has just been linked with the idea of a shop as indicated by the words next to it. In fact, if we have never been there we have absolutely no idea what the shop looks like and must draw on our imagination of what a shop looks like.

The last point is important – what we do not know about an experience our mind tries to fill in from previous experiences.

This does make distrusting your mind easy when you realise that if you had bad experiences with something – e.g. dogs - then your mind is going to try and steer you away from anything it considers similar. And your mind will look for similar experiences unless you consciously tell it that this new experience is not the same!

*Your mind is a system of thoughts which you can mentally step away from and observe. When you know your thoughts are observable and therefore NOT YOU then you are free.*

If you believe or even 'know' you cannot do this *you have simply been suckered by your mind.* The Matrix has you.

Understand, with everything I am saying here your mind will try to stop your observing it and changing it. It is a self-propagating self-preserving system. Like any living thing your thoughts do not want to die and they do not want to change. Thus they make you feel like they are true.

There is a fish that injects a paralyzing agent into the skin of its victim so that the victim does not feel its insides being sucked out! Your mind, your EGO wants to paralyse you from questioning it *unless* you train it to do so – and then it will feel wrong NOT to question your assumptions. That can be a good place to get to.

But when you convince yourself of this – when you logically think through the things I am saying and evaluate them for truthfulness – you will be willing to step away from your thoughts and ask: Is that really true? Objectively?

If it's not true, what do I desire to think instead?

Let me leave this section with a logical thought which I hope will persuade you to re-evaluate as many of your thoughts as you can find.

Many of the thoughts, and many of the connections you made about life: what *causes* what, what *means* what **were made as a child**.

Have you heard some of the nonsense that comes out of a child's mouth?

They don't make sense yet this is the time that many of your beliefs about life were formed! Yes... exactly!

So unless you have thoroughly examined and updated your childish beliefs (like 'life should be fair' and 'people should be nice') then, deep down, you probably believe some weird and frankly unrealistic stuff.

My weird belief (which took me years to figure out) was that I would be motivated by convincing myself I had nothing. And if I had nothing then it would motivate me to get *something*. Hmm. Given what we now know about the law of attraction/creation all it did was give me more thoughts of nothing – which I became very unhappy about! I couldn't enjoy my victories or celebrate what was already in my life because my mind kept resetting the value counter to zero!

Once I realized the stupidness of this belief – which is sometimes all it takes to change – I started counting my blessings – and believing the answers! You can do the same.

# Five: The Ego has to GO!

It's best for me to be up front about my definition of 'the EGO'. I am not referring to some Freudian sex and death monster (*eros* and *Thanatos*) who wants you to sleep with your mother and kill your father (yes, Freud said that).

I am referring to what you may variously call:

- The inner critic
- The critical inner voice
- The internal saboteur
- The Gremlin

Basically, it's the part of you that tells you that you can't do it and you should be scared to try anything new because it's dangerous. And because it talks to you it seems like a separate part of you watching out for you.

Well, actually the EGO is trying to protect you in the same way a person with a bad phobia of lifts would not want you to get in a lift. It's only source of information is the past and what you have failed at (primarily) and it's terrified of anything new. NEW=UNKNOWN, UNKNOWN=BADDDD!

But lifts help you get where you want to go and faster - and without new learnings you won't be going anywhere!

It can be hard to accept that part of you is actually working *against* your own best interests even though it thinks it is. It's like a friend pointing out all your faults so you'll have a 'realistic view of yourself'. We have a saying in England: 'With friends like that, who needs enemies?'

Your EGO does not help you. Essentially, it conjures up a negative image of yourself and then convinces you that this is how you truly see yourself. It hides the fact that IT is the creator and projector of your toxic feelings.

As Guy Finlay says: 'Just as the physical eye that sees can't see itself other than through a reflection you cannot see your psychological self other than by gazing at those mental images of your own creation. **So when seeing a failure in your mind's eye just remember in that moment who it is that put it there [YOU!]**

When you feel miserable – WHO PUT THE IMAGE THERE? WHO MADE THE FEELING AND SAID THE WORDS TO YOURSELF/ **YOU DID!**

**You see, the pictures and voices and feelings that come from within you seem to be a friend. They sound like you. But they are not you!** There is a mechanical process going on inside you that presents you with situations from the past. That's it's job and sometimes it does that job well.

But to use one of Guy's metaphor your consciousness is like Sleeping Beauty in the castle. Sleeping Beauty is your higher consciousness who may be currently asleep and the servants (memories, ego) are running the castle (YOU!) I know it sounds somewhat old-fashioned but these particular servants *need to know their place!* Wake up and take control so that they can do the job they are assigned to do **and nothing more**.

Your EGO is working against your best interests even as it insists (and is probably convinced) that it is working FOR them!

The best strategy to beat it is to consciously realise that every new moment is a moment where something new can be created by you. The EGO only works off the past – and the new moment is a place of potential – as you enter it you'll feel some aspect of the older you trying to suck you into defining what this NEW moment will be like.

But realise – it cannot! If you just let the new moment play out without having to name or judge it – you'll feel yourself entering into a freedom that comes from the present moment.

You will probably fail many times and fall back into your old thinking patterns – but as I said in the first quote – realizing how easy it is for you to be asleep can wake you up to how much you need to be more vigilant.

## SIX: OWN your Mind or it will be MINED

Who owns your mind?

I know, stupid question. It's yours.

Or is it?

Can you *honestly* say that your mind with all its funny behaviours is actually owned - and run - by you? I realize logically it is your mind. But do you really believe it? Do you know it?

Let's tackle this another way: what part of your body is 100% yours? A part you would never part with? Your heart? Your eyes? Your tongue? How strongly do you feel that's yours?

My bet is very strongly. In fact, if you think about someone trying to take any of those things away from you... can you feel that strong throaty **NO** coming? Because those things (or whatever you chose) are part of YOU and you have chosen OWNERSHIP over them. They are yours.

But when it comes to the mind we often feel like it runs us! As the book title goes: '*Emotions – sometimes I have them and sometimes they have me!*'

Imagine the grey matter of your brain. If we assume for a moment that the mind resides in the brain (and I realise there is a lot of debate on that) and that we need a brain to *experience* our mind then - if we feel the same strength of ownership for the grey and white matter inside our skull as we do our heart then that should change the way we feel about WHO actually runs it.

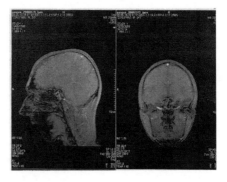

If it is MY brain and everything I feed it *is up to me*. So if **I** feed it depressing thoughts and images then that is what I get back. It and everything in it belongs to me but actually accepting that can be **hard**.

However, …. the moment I realized that I was responsible for the content of my mind was a chilling moment - and a liberating one. 'Chilling' because it meant that any negative rubbish left in my mind would be there until I chose to take the time to root it out; liberating because it meant I could actually program my mind with the thoughts and actions of a better life – and *that* was an exciting thought.

It was the following quote that made me finally decide to take ownership of my thoughts.

"The only person I am in competition with is myself."

This meant that **I** was the initiating cause of all the things I thought (secretly) that people were doing to me: all the 'you MADE me' (cause=effect) thoughts I had were actually just *me* forgetting that I was talking to myself, hurting myself - and thinking it was someone else doing it!

This means that when we feel victimized, we are victimizing ourselves ultimately. I mean really - who else is doing it? Are other people really reaching into our brains and MAKING us do stuff?

Quite literally despite it feeling like other people have SOOO much influence in our lives they actually have Jack. Nada. None. Not when it really comes to it. Nope, even with a gun to our head we have a choice. The victims amongst you will argue we don't – but we do. Stop wanting other people to save you – they are just trying to save themselves as well.

Read this post for an enjoyable take on letting others opinions run your life:

http://waitbutwhy.com/2014/06/taming-mammoth-let-peoples-opinions-run-life.html

**I want you to stop and ask yourself this question:**

*How exactly can someone else's opinion FORCE me to change my opinion of myself? To change my relationship with myself?*

I hope you realise this is a rhetorical question: one that has an obvious answer although if you are a people pleaser *the right answer will not FEEL obvious*.

You KNOW the Truth is that it can't. But you feel that it can. And for many people, that feeling is the last word for them. Feelings rule, thoughts drool.

The beginning of true wisdom is to be able to over-ride your thoughts: to act in spite of them not simply because of them.

Right now as I write this on a cold May morning I'm actually feeling pretty miserable. Why? Not sure but the point is that as I have learned to observe my feelings and not take them too seriously I am still writing to you. And realizing that, I feel happy! Those thoughts and feelings will pass like clouds in front of the sun. Plus I need to eat… all these other circumstances I have considered before I dive in and wrongly conclude I AM miserable. Too much effort for you? With practice, it won't be.

Anyway, back to the question I asked you: did you ask it just once? Did you then secretly conclude that although you intellectually *know* you cannot be forced to change your opinion of yourself based on others actions – you still will?

Come on, let's be brave and truthful here.

For reasons best known to you: you have agreed to put what you perceive as other's opinions above your own. For me there have been several reasons:

a) At one point I secretly thought other people were always right about me and I was wrong
b) I was bullied a LOT in my younger life and it became easier to give in than face aggravation day after day.

But I still agreed to it – and with lots of repetition established it in my mind as a pattern. So my intellect says 'yes' but my established habit says 'still people please'?

I advise you to keep returning to the question:

*How exactly can someone else's opinion FORCE me to change my opinion of myself? To change my relationship with myself?*

Going back to it again and again you will come up with reasons why saying 'YES' is not only wrong but repulsive. You'll begin to change your way of thinking and responding. You might get an instant change but more likely you'll feel less and less conflicted as the old pattern falls into disrepair.

I know lots of self-help stuff promises magic bullets of instant cure (and to be fair – there are methods in Neurosemantics and NLP and EFT) they do produce instant results. But behavioral and mental change still need to keep happening so you don't fall back into old patterns.

If you are working to change and going through hell – keep going. Someone once said that change is not just stopping climbing one mountain – it is about building a new one. So feel the crappy feeling, and do something else anyway. EVERY time you do – regardless of how it feels – you are building a new mountain grain by grain.

**No one can harm you unless you give them permission to do so. When you know that you run your brain and can change the thoughts in it to ones that empower you then you will become freer that you have ever been.**

## STOP AND THINK

The following process is a mental exercise that can help you feel the sense of ownership that I talked about above.

### The Ownership Pattern (by Michael Hall and Bobby Bodenhammer).

Please do the following:

1. What do you believe that you wish you didn't?

Can you objectively agree that that belief is irrational or unnecessary? At the least can you agree you'd be better off without it?

When you have you answer, write it down, set it aside for a moment.

2. Think about something you feel is totally and absolutely 100% yours:
- Your heart

- Your tongue
- Some other body part or personal possession
- Your child?

Ask yourself: How would I feel and act if someone wanted to take this away from me? Could they have it?

If this doesn't work, ask yourself: Would you push a child in front of a bus?

3. How fully now do you want to express that 'No' or 'NO WAY'!

Act it out, gesture your 'No!" Punch the air, push it away and shout 'No' with all your might. Feel the power of your 'No'. Get more and more aggressive and angry. Beat your chest. Roar. (Tip: close the windows so you don't scare the neighbors!')

4. Bring back to mind the beliefs you have about yourself, your abilities etc.

Direct the full power of your 'No' at that thought. Think about the negative beliefs and shout 'No' at it three, four, six times – keep repeating the 'No' until you feel its power start to weaken. Simultaneously punch out, push it away, stamp your feel – whatever most represents rejection to you.

Once you feel it weaken – and I cannot be more descriptive than that because it will feel differently for each person – take a 20 minute break. Wash up. Have a coffee.

5. Then you can ask yourself: What do I desire to believe instead?

Make a list. Imagine yourself speaking, acting and thinking using this new idea. Does it seem to fit?

If so, then find something you own or believe that you can say absolute YES to!

Psyche yourself up in a similar way. How big a 'YES' can you say to this?

Jump with joy, wave your arms – what do you do to celebrate and rejoice?

6. When you feel that with every fiber of your being direct your 'YES' at the thought you want to permanently say 'YES' to.

Say' YES YES YES YES! (I know what it looks like!) until you feel that thought begin to turn into something you know you believe. You will know when you feel it's 'true' or when your mind's voice starts saying 'of course I believe it'.

If you want to read the source material for this exercise go here:

---

Interestingly, if you make the above work then step back and think for a moment.

*You made yourself believe something*. No-one made you – *you made yourself believe something.*

There may not have been any outside evidence to prove whether the belief was objectively true or not – you simply applied more immediate emotional energy to a thought than you usually do. This is one way beliefs are created. It's not hard to understand if you think about how phobias are created – a one-time shock (e.g. spider on the face) produces a massive jolt of mental energy and BANG – a strong anti-reaction to spiders from there on. You created a belief that you MUST move away from spiders. So why not use that process on purpose?

(If it doesn't work - there is nothing *wrong* with you, it simply means there are some higher level beliefs preventing the change and that is beyond the scope of this book – see www.neurosemantics.com to learn how to address this. There's a steep learning curve and lots of practice involved but it's worth it.

# Seven: The danger of mental comfort

When you've been thinking the same thoughts for a while several things happen:

- The thoughts stabilise
- They naturalise
- They become familiar
- They become comfortable (even the uncomfortable ones)

Basically, it seems like you *always* thought that way. This can be very bad news.

Your mind is designed to reinforce what you already believe. The technical term for it is 'homeostasis' – meaning that your brain-mind-nervous system gets used to doing something repeatedly and then starts to use it as a reference point. It becomes established. It becomes comfortable. Automatic.

This is all very well when it comes to tying your shoelaces but not so good when it comes to hating yourself or being negative about some aspect of yourself.

You may think you want to change but you WILL at some point be tempted to think 'I don't want to change because I've always thought that way'. You may not voice it so precisely up-front but unless you acknowledge and deal with it, it will be like a little stone in the shoe of your mind.

- What negative thoughts do you habitually think against yourself?
- What are you ashamed of?
- What about your life/character/actions do you dislike?
- What do you do automatically do to sabotage yourself? What do you do so often that you hadn't even considered it sabotage?

**STOP AND THINK**: Write a few answers down. Look at them. How does doing them feel (not how do you feel afterwards, actually *when* you are doing/thinking them?)

- Familiar?
- Natural
- Part of you?

Stop. I mean, really STOP and ask yourself:

- Is stability and familiarity enough of a benefit to justify what these thoughts do to me/for me?

STOP AND THINK

For instance, if you are afraid to speak up with family members (and I have been through this one) then failing to speak up yet again may result in the thought: 'I've always been this way. This is the way I am.'

Wait.

Is the 'reward'* of stability and familiarity *really* reward enough to counteract the shame, the self-annoyance or whatever you feel about it reward enough simply because... it's comfortable and common for you to think that way?

We tend to associate comfort with pleasure. And "as a man thinketh", says the Bible, "so HE is". Notice it doesn't say 'If a man is comfortable with his thinking that makes it true.'

It does not. It simply means you repeated a lie until you believed it. And now you have trouble believing that you once didn't believe it. Because now you do!

***Comfort with inaccurate thoughts is an enemy of your progress.***

You need to get uncomfortable at the idea of consistency especially where negative thoughts are concerned. You need to find a *positive use of doubt*. More on this later.

I realized recently after YEARS of being blind to it that I over-valued the familiarity of being faithless and negative when a situation arose that seemed 'bad' and didn't have an obvious solution. I had placed more value on familiar and comfortable unhappiness and less value on the potentially unknown – but potentially better and more positive – future I could start to build in my head. One day, using the gestalt swap ideas elsewhere in this book I decided to start valuing a little kernel of positivity. I decided to prefer it, probably because I was sick and tired of negativity. And you know what? I feel like a closed door has started to open and the light of joy has started to peek through. I want more. You can have it to if you decide it.

You see - being comfortable with how you think provides all kinds of benefits... until it doesn't.

**It is entirely possible and utterly likely that you are comfortable with destructive and toxic thoughts about yourself.**

Without realising it you use a mental formula that says 'thought been there a long time = true'. Oh dear.

Even if you step back for just a moment you're starting to see the fallacy of that one, aren't you?

Let's deal briefly with the issue of Truth.

I'm going to suggest that in the objective world outside of ourselves Truth is what corresponds with Reality. Bridges are built because the properties of steel and concrete are known plus their tolerances and these qualities – their Truths – can be worked with in Reality. Yes, certain situations affect the way these materials behave but those circumstances are also Truth.

In the spiritual realm - if there is a God - then there are Truths about Him. Whatever we make up He will operate according to His own qualities and those will be the Truth. Whether He is Allah, Yahweh, Christ or some other deity. Whether we can know those Truths or not is a matter for much debate, just not here although it does tick me off when people say: 'Oh, that's just your belief' as in 'because I don't believe it, it doesn't exist'. Grow up. Go run into a tree that you don't believe in and *then* come back to me.

THEN… there are human 'truths'. As before, I'm going to rework the term psychology here into two words: LOGIC and PSYCH. Psychology is the LOGIC of the PSYCHE – your mind - and that logic is very rarely like 2+2=4.

That's what makes watching Mr Spock and Dr Mccoy of Star Trek so amusing… Spock is almost entirely logical which leads to decisions which really upset Dr Bones because to a human there are many shades of grey along with the black and white of logic.

Humans can connect almost any X with Y and make it truth.

- The way she looked at me **means** she likes me.
- The way she looks at me **means** she doesn't like me.
- I am afraid of feathers; **if** I touch them germs will swarm onto me.
- My god says I must kill those who don't believe in him **for me** to go to heaven.

- My god says I must let those who wish to kill me do so in order to go to heaven.
- Being rich will solve all my problems.
- Being poor will ensure I don't have the problems of the rich.
  And so on…!

Humans will make and follow all kinds of ideas.

These ideas become TRUE in our nervous systems. Richard Bandler, co-creator of NLP called beliefs 'commands to the nervous system'. So your mind treats something you believe as utterly True. And it will operate that way, sending commands to get you to try and live in accordance with that.

For years I believed that raised voices **meant** someone was coming to hurt me. Stupid? Well, it did mean that in my childhood home and it became 'my truth'. The problem was that years later it was still My Truth and even though the evidence around me no longer supported that conclusion my mind-brain didn't care. It was still true and I still flinched at opening doors and raised voices.

This is just one example of why comfort and familiarity with a belief does not make it automatically true.

It feels real. And in your body and mind it IS real. But you must get it into your head for this to work:

IT IS NOT OBJECTIVELY REAL

…and therefore any belief that directs your thinking and behavior in important areas needs to be checked for accuracy. Question yourself: Is this really objectively true? Is it? Really? Who would I be if I didn't have this belief? Happier?

Let me give you one other example of believing a destructive belief as true. I don't mind self-disclosing because I know we all have some messed up ideas, right?

I used to spend on impulse, driven by the deep conviction that 'I'll sort it out later because the money's going to come'. Well, yes, that is commendable to some extent but the effect of spending little and often is that the little debt becomes a big debt.

The belief is always stuck at the stage of 'I'll sort it out later' and never at the 'later' stage. Why? Because beliefs are only ever concerned with their own immediate agenda. They loop, self-reference and *only listen to their own 'voice'*.

Why do you think people who have one-night stands slink away in the morning? Because the beliefs they had about wanting sex NOW did not consider what you would do the next morning? And if she gets pregnant? A 'I want sex-NOW' belief would NEVER consider that by itself. You'd have to have another belief which was 'I'd better not do this or be very careful in case of pregnancy'. Not that I am advocating casual sex before marriage by the way.

## STOP AND THINK

Think of something you want to change about yourself or a belief that you 'wish' wasn't true. Relax into your Silence (see Chapter 2) and ask yourself:

- What if it were true that this belief only ever support itself?
- Is there alternative evidence for it not being true?
- And most importantly: what if I didn't have to believe this?

What you need to believe…no, scrap that… KNOW is that your thoughts can be changed because they only have the *appearance* of truth. Yes, they look true, feel true, and sound true and that is a problem… waiting to be solved.

Your thoughts are like the people who chose to see the emperor's new clothes. Actually, there was nothing there but they convinced themselves there was. You have gone a stage further. You were not born with the idea that you hated yourself. Is any beautiful new baby? Yet you convinced yourself then forgot you were the one who did!

Thankfully, God has given you the gift of conscious thought – and you're going to have to use it. Henry Ford said that 'thought is hard work which is why most men avoid it'. But I am here to tell you that the hard road [of thought] is actually the easy road [of building a better life]

Put in the effort now and you will truly reap what you sow.

### Activity

A great tool for breaking down beliefs is the META-MODEL questions by Richard Bandler and John Grinder. These questions force a person to be more specific about what they are referring to and as beliefs are very rarely specific they begin to totter and fall when seriously questioned:

Sample questions to ask something you believe about yourself:

- How does that work exactly? How do you get from X to Y?
- How do you know?
- What specifically do you mean? What specifically does that refer to?
- According to whom?
- Never? Never ever?

If you aggressively ask these questions of your belief **again and again** you will feel a shift in belief. You can learn more about the meta-model questions online.

http://nlp-now.co.uk/use-nlp-meta-model/

*(Yes, I said reward because the mind always rewards us for doing what we deep down think is 'right'). This is known as the theory of positive intent, the idea that our mind is always trying to do something positive for us even if the behaviours it uses are clearly not positive. A classic example is of the woman who kills her abusive husband to be free of him. Positive behavior? No. Positive intention – to be free.

# Eight: The positive uses of doubt

Did you ever think doubt could be a useful tool? Well it can. Lawyers think so. Okay, maybe not the best example but they introduce doubt into their questioning to undermine belief in the accuracy of a witness statement. They suggest to the jury indirectly that what the client says should not be 100% believed.

> What is the difference between a lawyer and a crayfish?
>
> One is a scum-sucking bottom feeder and the other is just a fish.

If you imagine that something you are sure is true about yourself, it is like a mini personal conviction and you'll never get it to **perjure** itself!

This term **perjure** is a legal one for when a witness is lying on the stand. The belief will *never* lie about itself as its very existence depends on you believing it! If you say 'Do I really have to reject my good ideas in the presence of my boss?' it will say YES - if that is what you already believe.

You need to attack it with questions that start to make it lose confidence, to doubt its own self-righteousness. Beliefs seem unassailable and unquestionable... until they are not. But they will not give in easily.

I strongly suggest (as I did above) you go online, type in 'meta model questions' and learn some of the questions of the NLP Metal model which can explode beliefs into dust bunnies faster than you can say 'hey presto'!

But back to the use of doubt. So again, here are some meta-model questions plus a few more to help you break down the Jericho walls of a belief:

So, pick something you don't like about yourself:

- I believe I can't....
- I'm no good at...
- I feel X (pick something negative) about Y (some aspect of your personality, appearance etc)

Once you have this in mind or have written it down concentrate, step back in your mind, and ask the following questions:

Do I think and feel this way ALL the time? In every context?

- When do I not think/feel/behave this way? Does that mean it's NOT true all the time?
- Who says it's true? What authority do they have? Do they truly know me better than myself? Did I give them the authority to sell me this idea?
- Who really decides what I believe about myself? If I say someone else HOW specifically do they do this? If I say 'they make me' then where are the buttons that they actually press? What do they do to take control of my personality?
- Is it possible that I choose to respond this way and then deny I am choosing? (that one might annoy you but ask it… stop and consider).
- How specifically do I prove that belief is true? What would make it not true? Does everyone believe this?
- What if this belief was gone? Was I born with it? If not, when did I learn it?
- When did I make this decision to believe this? Was I old enough to consider all the evidence or did I just believe because someone told me?
- How certain am I on a scale of 1-10? Am I SO certain, that I should actually be disturbed by my certainty? Am I certain enough to be uncertain?
- What if I doubted the truth of this 5%? 10% 45% What would that doubt open up for me to believe instead?
- What if I woke up tomorrow morning and this belief was gone? How would I feel? What would be there instead? What would I desire to be there instead?

These questions will probably give you a greater taste of what meta-modelling (the asking of the meta-model questions) can do for you.

**Believing your beliefs**

Although a complete treatment of this process (believing your beliefs) is beyond what I aim for in this book, it is an important part of understanding how your mind lies to you. In fact, it is so important because *without it being pointed out you'll probably never see it!*

Remember in the chapter on 'stepping back' in your mind I told you then when you think about another thought you:

a) Step back and step up in your mind to a conceptual position of looking down on it (or thinking 'about it' from a higher perspective)

b) Enter the position of power from where you can make a decision about those lower thoughts.

A bit like this (start reading at the bottom of the diagram and read upwards):

**Current thinking from higher position**

**ME CONSCIOUSLY CONSIDERING@ (about)**

**/ FIRST THOUGHT \\**

Technically, a belief can be thought of as a solidified thought – a thought that has received enough emotional energy to stabilise and start reproducing the effects of itself in your mind and your life rather than just being blown away by the next thought.

It's also easy enough to gauge if you believe something: Just ask yourself: "Do I believe that x is true?"

- Do I believe there is a strawberry on the Eiffel tower?
- Do I believe that sex before marriage is okay?
- Do I believe in God?
- Do I believe the vanilla ice cream is better than chocolate?

… and so on

However…. It is not so easy to check *if you believe in your beliefs*.

What's that?

It's one thing to believe that, for example, it's wrong to eat meat but it's quite another to believe in the rightness of the belief. It's not easy to explain but just as shouting down a tunnel can amplify the sound waves of your voice, so believing in a belief increases its believability by a huge factor.

**/I believe I am totally right to believe in the evil of eating meat \\ (BELIEF ABOUT BELIEF)@**

**/ Yes, it's wrong to eat meat /@ (BELIEF about)**

**/ MEAT \\ (on the table)**

I'm going to share something very disturbing. This is how fundamentalists think:

They don't just believe they are right – they believe in the rightness of their rightness so much that no other thoughts can possibly get in.

Now before you start with: 'I always *knew* there was something wrong with those religious folk – STOP it!' Anyone can be fundamentalist, - believing in the rightness of their beliefs to the point of blind stubbornness. Have you ever met a fundamentalist vegan? Feminist? Democrat? Pro-life? Pro-choice? Aliens on Hayley Bob?

You also have fundamental beliefs – the ones about yourself you never think to question. I recently got annoyed at a relative for constantly posting sarcastic comments on my Facebook profile. When I challenged her about it… she had no idea what I was talking about because it was just habitual and normal to her.

How do you spot toxic or unhealthy areas in your life? Look at your results? Are your surrounded by negative people? Could it be because you are a negative moaner as well? Maybe not, but consider it.

Are you overweight? What are your beliefs about exercising and diet? Do you never question your junk food intake (feeling guilty now…)

If you really cannot see areas for improvement - Ask someone you trust – what do you see in me as my worst faults?

Once you wake up to the white noise of your insecurity, negativity etc, that was always there you can start questioning them *no matter how normal they feel*:

So how do you break such a thinking pattern?

The answer is laughably simple. So simple it took me 17 years to figure out.

You simply need to realise you are doing it. Often, realizing the stupidity of believing in something that is often, at most, an opinion is enough to destroy it for good. Really.

But first you *must* consider the idea that beliefs are not objectively true and most do not refer to an objective truth. How can they? Forget how they feel for a minute because often that's all you are basing your 'believing' on.

A belief is nothing more than a chemical structure processed by electricity in your mind-brain. How can it be anything else? Yet when we are *in* the belief it is like we are in the Matrix – it is our truth.

When you consider it's physical nature and step back you can ask :

Do you believe the truth of that 'truth?'

Is it really objectively true?

When I scrutinize it can I say that this is based on some objective standard of truth? For example, you can establish the physical properties of steel and consider those 'truth' for how the material behaves. But you can find any objective and totally Truthful standard for your value? As a believer I would say 'yes', from God but if you're not interested in that you can still say: 'Well, no-one on earth has divine power to know all of me – and measure all of my value – so actually no, the belief that I am worthless cannot be verified. I do not have to believe that belief.

Is it objectively true that everyone hates me? Where's my proof?

I believed it but do I need to believe in that belief?

At some point (and I cannot honestly say when) you will realise that you are believing *real-lies*.

I'm going to share one of the beliefs I broke using this process...

**"I don't have an opinion – my very existence is threatened by disagreement. I will be annihilated and not survive if I disagree."**

As I have said before, I realise how stupid these beliefs can look and seem if you don't have anything like them but this one caused me to people please for over thirty years. I didn't realized that I not only believed it but was sure and certain it was true.

That second level of belief (the sure and certain part) was hidden from my understanding in my unconscious mind and was powering and driving my everyday behavior. I used to feel so ashamed when I was found myself saying and doing things to get people to approve of me – it was like an addiction.

But when I said to myself: "I believe that my existence is threatened but is it actually? This *is just a belief, right*? I have believed that belief but if I stop believing that belief, I'll be free. If I stop believing the framework that powers it then it has no power, right?"

And at that moment, I burst out laughing and was freed. Just like that. Thirty years of mental imprisonment gone and I felt light as a feather.

One thing you will discover is how quickly your mind reorganizes itself around your new perceptions. So the moment you decide that, for example, 'I don't know that his expression means he hates me' you will most probably:

a) Feel a sense of relief
b) Feel like you always believed the new perception

Just step back and observe that process for a moment. It is a momentary glimpse of a system designed to protect itself – by presuming to you that it contains no lies. Your mind, my friend, has just momentarily show HOW it lies to you.

# Nine: A little time out for a friendly cigar...

Becoming aware of the kind of thoughts you have, even the ENERGY of your thoughts is kind of like becoming aware of air. It's hard. Air is just there and unless it is blowing in your face you don't notice it.

Plus you need to have a good reason to convince your mind to question itself. It's not designed to do that. It's designed to reinforce and backup the way you think. Oh, it and it will help you hide things you think about yourself that you don't like to think you think!

So when you start exploring your mental landscape you will find you don't like some of what you find! Especially if you think of yourself as a fairly logical, kind and 'good' person you might be surprised at some of the really nasty and weird stuff you find in your head. Of course, *you* won't find anything but I sure did. Here's a few examples:

I had connected budgeting with poverty and for literally decades I could not understand why I didn't want anything to do with budgeting. A little more thought revealed to me that many of the people my mother was friends with were bitter and desperate and angry – and money was often mentioned in that context. In other words, as a child I thought managing money was something to be miserable around! No wonder I didn't want to manage it.

Once I had understood this I was able to redefine budgeting as 'part of wealth creation', 'resource allocation' and 'being in control' all things that I value!

> I would like to remind you that your mind seeks to real-ize – make real whatever thoughts you have. So as Andy Shaw says EVERYTHING you think is either helping you or hurting you. There is no grey area – no holding area of indecision.

I'd also connected 'confronting others' with survival and 'possible death'. Yes, you can laugh if you want to but if you're struggling with a particular habit you can't give up be sure there's something deep (or high!) inside driving it.

I was talking to a friend a few days ago who drinks up to 8 litres of Pepsi Max *a day*. A problem, wouldn't you say? He was also sleeping a lot and not going out, losing days. Did I think he was depressed? he asked me. I suggested that he might be but also that dosing himself with junk food was something I used to do to avoid being alone with my thoughts. He agreed he might be doing this too.

Our minds don't have grey areas. No matter what we deny to ourselves any thoughts that are in there are either helping us or hurting us. Full stop. We need to know so we can conquer it. As the proverb says 'He who conquers a city is mighty but he who conquers himself is mightier still.'

So you now have some ideas about how to find some of what you believe. But how do you **deal** with what you find? Through Acceptance. Yes, little old seemingly innocuous *acceptance*. This state of mind is one major key to mind power and mental manifestation.

No, I am not going all New-Age and weird on you. Give me a chance and let me define why I mean by 'acceptance' and why it is so powerful.

Most people think the phrase 'just accept it' means 'give up and mope'.

What I mean by acceptance is more like *acknowledging* that something *exists* and by doing so it gives you the option to do something about it. More than that it gives the potential **POWER** to do something about it because until you acknowledge, for instance, that your thinking is prompting and helping you overspend, you cannot change it.

It can feel very… yucky… to accept you have some pretty unpleasant or even 'evil' thoughts about yourself and others. But you don't have to spiral off into self-pity about how bad YOU are.

Andy Shaw teaches that we should 'observe' our thoughts rather than try to change them.

I don't entirely agree that only observation works - but it is useful to get into the habit of watching our thoughts rather than get sucked into them. I love what Captain Jack Sparrow said in Pirates of the Caribbean: Dead Man's Chest when told there would come a moment when he would make a decision to do good:

'I love those moments. I like to wave at them as they go by' i.e. I am watching my thoughts and not acting on them!

Shaw points out that 'judgement is weakness, observation is power' and what he means by this is that when we are observing our thoughts we are actually changing them purely through the act of observation. Physicists have known this for year – that merely watching an experiment alters the way things perform – they call it the observer effect.

But I have found that when becoming aware of thoughts that previously would suck you into judging yourself, stepping back and 'watching the fireworks' does tend to take away their power to 'compel'. So next time you feel the negativity coming on tell yourself: 'I'm taking a step back now' and just watch yourself.

(More on this in the 2x2 process chapter.)

**Acceptance is better than doubt because doubt kills creativity**

Do you struggle with doubting yourself a lot? Do you really need doubt as a thinking process? Do you actually need to second-guess and question whether something will really work? Do you need to be plagued by opposing thoughts and indecision?

At one time, I thought 'yes'. I thought doubt was just part of our normal thinking processes. In fact, I thought, as I think many of you do that if I did NOT doubt then I would be caught out and miss something important!

However… when it comes to evaluating the pros and cons, and what will and won't work – can't you do an as-good or better job *without doubt*? I mean, if you're thinking processes were working on potential solutions for all aspects of the situation and you do your due diligence - would you not cover the same ground? And in a more pleasant way?

Take booking a holiday. How does doubt serve you there?

You need to decide a destination, book hotels (if that is your thing), appropriate transport. You need the right clothes, passports, insurance if you want it and possibly check up on how to best interact with the locals with a Lonely Planet Guide or someone who has been there before. And so on. How does doubt help you achieve any of that if you are fully thinking the situation through.

'Ah, but doubt makes me realise something I might have missed.' That may be true but a careful evaluation of what you need to consider and include *can do the same job as doubt*!!!

If it is true that any thought either helps you or harms you then doubt is an insidious parasite that feeds off your mental energy and take away from the creative process. It's like a mental stone in your shoe!

When we are referring to bigger projects: building a house, moving overseas, saving the planet – *you can still evaluate your resources and strategies without doubt!*

The next time you doubt something just observe and see if the information it is giving you is:

a) Useful
b) Could have been discovered without doubt!

If you keep doing this then you can train your mind to find solutions and eliminate the pains of doubt. For a much fuller treatment on this read Andy Shaw's Bug Free Mind books.

**Anxiety**

In the same way anxiety is about the future. Let me tell you something. You won't like it but it is possibly the most adult, mature and useful thing you'll hear all day.

**Some things are going to happen whether you like it or not.**

You can do the following:

Prepare as best as you can to handle the situation which you will then HANDLE as best you can when it arrives.

Accept there are some parts you cannot handle.

Your tears, tantrums and pleadings, denial and refusing to think about it *does not help*. It's like a kid rolling on the floor but his mother still won't buy the chocolate bar.

I am not saying we cannot influence or avoid situations but some things will happen.

For example, three days ago I asked a builder to seal a leak in the toilet. That would have cost £60/$87.

He declared some parts inside the tank needed replacing. So that was another £50.

I misunderstood what he said about not using the toilet at-all for 24 hours and the seals broke. So that was another £120 for labor and quick drying sealant. Then today, my son flushed the toilet and the tank split down the back gushing liters of water on the floor....

I do not have the money to replace it today.

So for the next month we will pour water down the pan to flush all the nasties away. Why? Because this is life! What good would complaining and pulling my hair out do! I even had a good laugh at the irony of it all.

**Is refusal to accept/acknowledge stemming from an entitlement mentality?**

Have you ever cried or felt really down because things didn't work out the way you want? I have. Yes, big boys do cry.

To say it straight, I used to get depressed because I believed deep down I was entitled to a better life than I had and therefore, in some magic child-like way, reality had to bend to my will to deliver it to me.

Nowadays, I tend to tell myself:

a) Welcome to life
b) It'll all work out

I'll explain:

Despite all these New Age teacher telling you, you can design reality there can be times when things don't work out the way you want. No surprise there. Don't misunderstand me - I am open to the idea of things working out exactly the way I desire or at least in the way I need. But not for the reasons I once had!

When I was a child life was hard for me. I was bullied at home and bullied at school – life was truly the pits.

At some point I decided that I deserved a better life than this but instead of deciding to make reality my friend and work for me – by acknowledging where I was in life and working to improve it– I decided that I deserved special treatment because of how I had suffered.

Thus I reasoned albeit unconsciously that the rules – the learning curve - didn't apply to me and I just needed to find 'the shortcut to success'. Is any of this familiar to you? If you read a lot of self-help work it may be. If not, just skip to the next section.

Yes, I know it seems ridiculous but didn't you know 'ridiculous' and 'human logic' are often the same thing?! I spent thousands on self-help courses, especially those that promised painless routes to success. When one didn't work for me I'd move onto another without doing the groundwork necessary for success to build on it because I really thought it should be easier than it was. It was like self-help OCD and it wasn't until years later I worked out what was driving it.

I believed deep down there was a way to avoid the hard work and pain (as I perceived it then) involved in developing myself into a more capable person. If only I could find a hidden pathway that would enable me to get rich and not have to interact with a lot of people 'cause people were violent and brutal.

I was deluded but didn't know it which is the definition of deluded!

In short, I thought I was entitled to have reality bend to my will because my life had been hard blah blah blah! Well, life doesn't work that way.

Now you will discover, if you have not already, that perception plays a keen role in how you act in life and that is because of how you interpret it.

Right now, as I am writing this, there is a financial situation looming. I am waiting for a phone call which could actually lower my disposable income.

What I am doing? Well, after a few minutes of freaking out I recall my principles (and a quote from Star Ship Troopers: 'Remember your training and you will live through this!') and I start asking myself:

- How is this great?
- How is God working in all things for the good of love who love Him?'
- What is utterly fantastic (hands raised in the air!) about this?

After the usual reply of my ego – 'there's nothing good about it' – I come up with two things (ask you shall receive!).

1) It means I'll have to become more serious about financial discipline. Great, that will really be a good thing in the short and longer term
2) Thank God I actually have the money to meet this financial situation. If it were not there I'd be in real trouble So it's actually going to be fine.

**Of course, I have already said that acceptance of what is gives me more power than resisting 'reality'.**

---

Well, I have just had the phone-call and things are not as bad as I imagined. It reminds me of what Mark Twain, author of the book Tom Sawyer said: "I'm an old man, I've had many troubles, most of which have never happened…"

---

## Acceptance of Change

Someone once said: "The only certainty is uncertainty and the only constant in life is change".

If this is true – and I think it is – then for most people, it's a piece of bad news they just don't want to hear.

Constant change and uncertainty requires an expenditure of mental energy and an ongoing willingness to look at your beliefs and strategies for how you handle 'reality'.

In my experience most people don't respond well to the idea or the reality of change. Once we're settled in our beliefs about how the world works it usually takes a big shock to get us to re-examine what we believe.

Yet the world is changing rapidly.

From once seemingly inviolable moral standards that most agreed on across the spectrum to how business is done and won – you now cannot be certain of what the person next to you believes – and you cannot be sure that the way you did business last year will exist or be profitable next year.

Truly, the saying 'keep up or be left behind' applies to making it in the modern world. This is what forcing yourself to be conscious and awake to what is going on is so vitally importance.

Coming to terms with the fact that you cannot rest in your supreme personal knowledge of how the world really works – funny isn't it that 7 billion other people think the same thing! – is very destabilizing at first.

You may ask yourself: 'What can I rely on then if everything is always changing'. Well, slow down. Not everything changes. Basic human motivations for survival, socialization, recognition, and growth will always remain.

In my opinion the virtues of honesty, integrity, generosity and many other good qualities will never go out of fashion.

It's not that situations don't change – rather we need to internalize some core principles and be flexible in how to apply them.

When people know you keep your word you gain their trust and respect. When people know you will tell them the truth but in a way that is loving and compassionate – thanks wife – they will come to you for further guidance. If you are the 'ideas' person, then that will become your badge of honour.

Having said that – you still need to understand that not every culture values the same values that you do.

It's a trite example but in UK culture calling someone fat is usually taken as an insult. In Guyanese culture it's a compliment as it shows you are wealthy. My stepdaughter often told me 'Uncle, you look fat' and didn't understand when I acted insulted… because Guyanese women tend to like men with some meat on them. I am certainly not fat as in obese – but my belly has a certain roundness to it…

Your mind will lie to you and tell you to ignore changes, that they'll just go away, that 'you can't handle the truth' (yes, A Few Good Men!)

It is work and mental effort but you can – and you HAVE to! I am looking to generate four million pounds from products. Why should I not? There's no limitation on my dream, right?

In my pursuit of this I've had to become a lot tougher and more savvy in my dealings with people. I've had to learn to say less, listen more and insist on boundaries such as 'non-disclosure agreements'. I felt really awkward first as I was essentially telling people 'I don't trust you – sign this'.

But professional business people understand because there are dishonest people in the world who only fear being sued! So now I am willing to do it. I have also had to make the decision to stop working with certain people because our styles are just too incompatible. Ouch. I really don't like doing that. But I have changed and my dream will go on…. But unlike the Titanic – it will stay afloat!

How we respond to those changes is an interesting point for discussion. The first most important thing to look at is your personal response to the reality that other people – about seven billion of them – have a reality different to you!

I don't know an easy way to say this but truly:

**Acceptance is power. If you can deal with how the situation truly is you can respond to its reality and either accept that you cannot do something – or find that you can.**

This is not going to go down well when a situation is really awful. But acknowledging what is going on at least gives you some options.

Each time you face the reality of a situation you get a bit stronger. You also find out that the strength you desire is already within you.

# Ten: Why you want and need pain in your life

"Everything we do – is driven by you!"

Your brain

Do you want to create more pain in your life? More problems? More failure?

"Of course not" you say, 'who would?'

Except that you **do** and I'm going to prove it so you can see how you are contributing to your own sabotage.

You may not be happy after reading this but you *will be* better informed to stop mentally and emotionally punching yourself in the face.

Let's take a brief 'what if' tour. What if every part of your brain was working on your behalf to be helpful? What if, in the best scenario, every part of you was lined up and contributing to your success? If you read me asking this in an earlier chapter and did the exercise, you'll know it feels good to imagine that.

Now I realise it doesn't seem that way – after all – if you were all congruent and perfect you wouldn't have those bad habits, right? Picking your nose, over-spending, sexual-addition, drinking or just being negative all the time – come on, yes you do: we all have something we wish we didn't do.

What if I told you that it would be useful to assume that all of your behaviours and habits ARE working on your behalf? Even the ones that are really destructive. It would sound ridiculous, wouldn't it?

And yet if you take a step back and assume for a minute that everything you do has a positive intention behind it then it starts to make more sense.

Haven't you ever done something where you 'meant well' but you ended up hurting someone or being misunderstood? When you explain yourself to people you tell them that what *intended to do was good* but the action didn't reflect that so it just looked bad.

A classic example is when a battered woman (or man) lashes out at their partner and kills them. The intention was to protect themselves which in and of itself is 'positive' but the outcome is anything but.

I need to mention that positive here is not being used in the traditional usage. I do not mean 'sunny, happy, shiny' – the mind is simply trying to carry out an instruction it assumed was for your benefit. This is why I have said that any strongly held belief (whether positive or negative) is going to try and real-ize, make itself known in your life.

Your mind does not have a quality control mechanism of its own. Your stomach will try and vomit poison: your mind will try and make more of it! That is why the Old Testament proverb says : 'Be careful how you think: your thoughts determine your life' (TEV).

Let's get back to the main point. Your mind assumes that a strongly held (and thus strongly energized) belief is valuable and thus 'good' simply because it has lots of mental energy coming from it.

So logically if you have a strong belief that you are worthless, stupid, can't do maths, will never be loved or whatever then your mind believes you WANT the pain that goes with that. Yes, in its little mind-formula **energized belief=good and must manifest in my life** so it thinks that by manifesting even the most horrendously toxic beliefs *it is doing you a favor!*

If you get a chance read Addicted to Unhappiness. This revolutionary book reveals a source of self-sabotage that most of us might never recognize. The authors suggest that as children we thought our parents were always right. So if we had parents that consistently abused us verbally and/or physically then in our childish minds we believed they were right to do so.

Therefore, when we felt unhappy it was RIGHT to feel unhappy because this is how we made our parents – and therefore ourselves – happy.

Basically, we needed to be unhappy to be happy. This is a prime example of our minds thinking that something that feels bad – is good. This also explains why when we get to a certain level of achievement our minds might reference our childhood memories and cause us to sabotage ourselves or back off from success.

**This is where your mind is a liar!**

This is why, as I will say a thousand times if I have to, that you HAVE to decide to distrust your mind as a source of Truth. Because it so often isn't. Because those self-help teachers who tell you that our emotions are a source of truth (they aren't) and you are God (you really, really are not) are trying to get you to trust your mind more than it deserves.

Don't get me wrong – you need to trust your mind to work on your behalf when creating ideas, manifesting, and working things out – but you need to have a healthy suspicion for what it is assuming on your behalf!

So what can you do when your mind is trying to do good that is actually turning out bad?

Well, first you need to do away with the idea that there's something inherently wrong with you. It's not useful.

Think of yourself as a scientist investigating how a process works in a machine: your mind. Think of what answers will come to you as data, it helps you lessen the emotions that come with the answer.

- Think about this habit (thinking habit or behavior or both) and ask yourself:
- What could be a positive intention behind this?

Could this behavior be trying to protect me? Inspire me? Force me to express myself more fully? (These are just suggestions)

- Keep asking yourself the question regardless of whether you get an immediate answer. If you get no answer tell your mind 'you'll give me the answer by this time today – and pick a time. Then just forget about it and wait for the answer to come to you. Trust me. It will.
- Once you get an answer (which may be one word or a few) then ask yourself: What other (healthier) ways of honoring this intention? What other way of behaving would allow this intention to be fulfilled?
- What is this current behavior NOT allowing me to do that, if I could do it, would be a better way of behaving?

So let's say you are refusing to speak up at meetings and you find out the positive intention of your silence is to protect yourself from feeling embarrassed. Well, what is not speaking up doing for you? Not much, if you are being overlooked and negatively evaluated by co-workers for not contributing! So perhaps you would be better able to protect yourself by developing some speaking up behaviours? Perhaps speaking up would be better protection for you and more important than feeling embarrassed.

Doing such mental exercises is actually priming your brain to adopt new ways of thinking.

# Eleven: Emotions

It's difficult these days to say anything profound or new about emotions (as so much has already been written by others) but it is still possible to say something practical and perhaps dispel a few lies that bind.

I'm defining an emotion as something you feel and think about *simultaneously*. Perhaps it helps to think of it this way: physical warmth is a feeling; anger is an emotion because the emotion of anger is made up of angry thoughts and the feelings that come with the anger.

You may or may not be convinced by the idea of emotions being made up of thoughts and feelings but the fact that you are not aware of what you are thinking when you are feeling something speaks only about your current level of awareness.

It's like those people who say 'I don't see images' or 'I'm an auditory thinker'. What is actually true is that everyone has images, and sounds and smells and tastes *on the inside of their heads as well as on the outside*. You just might not be aware of it yet.

In fact, some developers in the field of emotional intelligence call emotions 'thoughts in the body' as our thoughts are expressed all over our physical body in the form of sensations and even illnesses.

These emotions, like beliefs, lie. They operate like they are always right. So if you feel righteously angry about something you'll continue to feel that way unless another piece of data comes in to contradict or transform that feeling. King Solomon, the wisest man who ever lived said 300 years ago: 'Every man is right in his own eyes'. And he was right. Both literally and in his own eyes ☺!

Heck, even when we feel wrong about something we are sure that we are right to feel wrong!

**This certainty is only true if the assumptions it's based on are accurate. Otherwise, it's just more lies.**

Have you ever seen someone 'blinded by love'? They simply cannot look at a situation objectively because the intensity of the feeling simply does not allow for any contradictory evidence.

Would it surprise you to know all emotions work this way whether you 'feel' them intensely or not? The thought process behind them is designed to reinforce the feelings of rightness you have about them.

You might say 'I don't feel right about hating myself' but actually your mind thinks you are right to do it. It's not very smart. It simply carries out the instruction you gave it to hate yourself and it will continue to do so unless you challenge it.

Remember what I said in an earlier chapter about the danger of familiarity – homeostasis occurs. You get used to feeling a certain way.

Furthermore, as Guy Finlay says, negative emotions give us a strong sense of who we are – **they created an identity of someone who suffers or who has been mistreated.** And, I believe, because we love familiarity more than change *we prefer to value known misery over unknown freedom*.

But are you tired enough of comfortably feeling bad about yourself? Are you prepared to take it on faith that no matter how engrained and unchangeable your negative emotion feels - it is still a lie? A lie with no proof it's a lie EXCEPT deep down you DO think more highly of yourself.

How do I know this?

Because if you had accepted the insults and warped thinking you heap upon yourself you would not be in such pain about it. You are made for something better. And it's the smallest mustard seed of hope that this is true that keeps you searching for answers.

> In that moment, it's not so much going with what "feels right" as it is basing your choice in seeing what is truly for you; **it's knowing without thinking about it that no negative state wants what is right for you.**
>
> **Guy Finlay**

We must have realized by now if the 'old' answers from our past (memories and experiences) are working for us. If they just cause us more pain then we need to be prepared to learn something new.

### A practical step

Elsewhere in this book you can find the 2x2 process by Ralph Cushnir. However, you may need to actually acknowledge/accept the presence of an unwanted emotion before you can let it wash through you.

The way to do this is simple. Think of something you totally and utterly accept and even welcome:

- A new baby
- A puppy/kitten
- A loved friend
- A sunset

You choose.

Then immerse yourself in a imagined experience of that thing. Allow the sunset to warm your face; hear the baby cooing and hold it in your arms; feel the love for a friend etc.

As you feel that let it become as strong as it can be – and then bring into your mind the emotion you previously avoided or rejected.

Let the acceptance flood onto and transform the negative emotion. Providing your acknowledgement/acceptance is strong enough you'll feel a shift – like something has given and moved.

Then, take a deep breath and think about that previously negative emotion. If you don't feel any different repeat the process a couple more times.

But what about my behavior you ask? I don't know what to do to stop triggering that feeling? The above will help. But how do you learn something new? By making a mess of it until you learn how not to… that's one way. It may not be the answer you want but it's a true one.

Or you can seek out the guidance of others who have walked the path before us AND can understand how our situation might differ from theirs. If you find someone like this, their advice can be gold dust.

We are so prepared to jump for the first answer that we think that any thought that automatically comes to mind is the right one. We must be prepared to say 'I don't understand' why I am feeling this because don't you see? That can open up space for a real answer instead of one that does not work. It's alright to say: 'I don't know' but I can learn.

Right now I am learning to deal with someone who I perceive as quite bossy and domineering. At first I just avoided them. Then I started to say: 'It's okay I don't understand how to deal with this'; 'It's okay that I don't understand clearly why I feel like this.'

This too, is acceptance. It makes room for some new answers, maybe even some truth. It's liberating.

**As Finlay says: "...new self-knowledge [which comes from not just accepting our old answers] enables us to win in life in a new way by revealing that the only time any event can defeat us**

# Twelve: Stop Blaming others: it's your own darn fault!

Until you take complete responsibility for yourself you will always be compromised as a human being. Your integrity and authenticity will be flawed – basically – you will be inauthentic and unless you have blocked yourself from feeling feelings of incongruence you will live with the uneasy knowledge that you are not being true to the values you really do hold.

I know, because I have thought and acted like *that* human being. But I also know it's easy to confess because virtually everyone else on the planet is like that too...

In this chapter I'm going to discuss fear of others, people pleasing and blaming others.

In these areas its particularly important to be convinced that you do lie to yourself because I want you to hear me (or read me) very carefully.

**The more control you can exert over what YOU do the more of your inherent power you can use.**

Note I did not say you can have power over others. I did not say you will be powerful or have unlimited power. The truth is that few people really know where their upper limits of achievement and ability are. So it seems a better goal to me to strive to find out, making certain assumptions along the way.

For example, I have assumed for years that my family genetics have little or no effect over my attitudes and dispositions. Now my birth mother got severely depressed after I was born and was placed in a psychiatric facility. I also have endured – and conquered - severe depression. But does that mean with absolute certainly that I inherited a 'depressed gene' from her? No. There's no proof. And assuming that 'depressing myself' is part of my genetic and unavoidable inheritance would tempt me to give up trying to make myself feel better.

I also would not have investigated Cognitive Therapy. I would not have trained as a Cognitive Behavioral coach. I would not have believed the message of the New Testament which says that change for the better is very possible and there is Divine assistance available. I would not have changed my life and influenced the lives of others for the better.

Even if there IS some influence from that 'gene' I would rather assume that **I** have the majority of the influence over my thoughts and feelings. So I set out to find out how much and, to my relief, I have been able to influence my attitudes a lot – which also led to the writing of this book many years later.

You can get to like being a victim. We can all take a perverse pleasure in our misery and this is to do with the way we can layer positive emotions onto and about a negative situation. We can like feeling bad and then deny that we like it but secretly still do!

How did I overcome this victim mentality? Well, although it's embarrassing to admit I eventually just got sick of it and started reading and learning from the work of others.

The more you learn about the way your mind might operate the more you can direct it yourself. I suppose the biggest learning came from understanding that negative states are more the result of habit than anything else.

The habit of negative thinking actually changes the structure of your brain – literally, brain tissues grows to support the habit of negative thinking. See the books *Brain Lock* or *You are Not Your Brain* by Jeffrey Swartz for photos proving this.

The books are basically about Obsessive Compulsive Disorder (OCD) but the author stresses the process he teaches works for almost any repetitive thoughts.

Basically, the more you fear the more you fear! You have to start 'going against the grain' and speaking, thinking and behaving in a different way EVEN WHILE your brain is trying to force you to repeat the old thought or behavior. Oh, it is uncomfortable.

I had a big problem with people pleasing for most of my life and when I started resisting the feelings that wanted me to seek approval it was mental agony. I just had to sit with it and repeat: That's not ME; it's just my brain' – and get on with something else unconnected to my brain's current desire.

The first step is to dis-identify with your mind – to understand that Descartes was wrong – we are NOT just our thinking ('I think therefore I am). Even if you think he was right – conceptually it is useful to separate the idea of the CORE of you from your thoughts.

Try repeating these sentences slowly to yourself- really STRESS the 'I'.

- I have thoughts but **I** *am not* my thoughts.
- I have emotions but **I** *am not* my emotions

- I say words but **I** *am not* my words.
- I have a body but **I** *am not* my body.

Do you feel the feeling of 'distance' or separation that creates, even briefly? This is because the YOU that observes these thoughts is NOT those thoughts. Call it consciousness, call it spirit but acknowledge it.

This is a taste of hope. Just because you spend most of the time feeling miserable and trapped in an emotion or thought does not mean you ARE trapped there. YOU are something different, a something that has simply learned to stay IN a feeling.

This is why observing one's thoughts is so useful. Because when you are observing them you are not in them.

# Thirteen: Fighting the Flooding Of Fierce Feelings

'If you are going through hell, keep going.'

Winston Churchill

For years, I lived in a constant state of fear. Deep down I was in pain, feeling I had failed as a father and was a worthless human being, craving approval from others. I also was terrified of conflict, fearing it would always turn into violence. The reasons don't matter; the feelings were real.

On the outside I put up a brave front. Most of the time I could summon the courage to say what I wanted to say, whilst shrinking inside. Friends would say I was brave and principled and I did some crazy things in support of my convictions. At times, though, through weakness and tiredness I would compromise and say what I thought the other person wanted to hear.

I felt 'flooded', so overwhelming were the feelings that I could barely think about behaving differently. My wife, bless her, would encourage me to speak God's Words over my life but at the time I could barely think for the intensity of anxiety. That's hard to understand unless you experience it.

One morning, after compromising by saying something different to what I thought inside, I had had enough. I sat down on the stairs alone and I cried, in fact, I howled with shame and tears and pain.

At that point I decided enough was enough. I had read *The One Thing Holding you Back* by Ralph Cushnir who had said the one thing I didn't want to hear: that the only way out of these emotions – was through them.

If you have studied personal development for a while and you suffer from debilitating fear you will certainly have tried lots of techniques that you think will help you solve fear, *whilst avoiding actually feeling it*. I have found that this generally... doesn't work.

As Susan Jeffers so famously said: 'Feel the fear and do it anyway.'

The secret is what some might call paradoxical: to **feel** the uncomfortable feelings AND simultaneously surround them with feelings of kindness and welcome.

The basic process is this: you find the trigger for what Cushnir calls 'the flinch' and rather than retreat from it you allow yourself to experience the full storm of emotion, staying with it until it subsides bringing brighter emotional skies on the other side.

You may be thinking 'Hot Damn!'; I'm not welcoming those feelings – do you know how painful they are? Soul-searingly painful, that's what!'

I understand this. I gave twenty years of avoiding certain feelings. But doing this will give you a new courage and a conviction that you can be in charge of your feelings and not the other way around.

Think of it logically: although your thoughts and feelings may tell you otherwise **you are designed to experience the full range of emotions**, including the rubbish ones! Your system will not break apart; you will not die. I know you think you will, you just **won't**.

You were designed to cope, you just never opened the emotional throttle to allow it all through so you feel untested. Well, it's a lie. You can feel it and survive. I have. It can be like standing in a giant emotional blow-torch – it can be emotional agony - but it *will and does* subside.

---

This may seem like just another spin on the arguments above but read it and consider for yourself. Most of the time we think we 'could not stand' feeling the negative and painful feelings we are avoiding. But actually we have already proved we can and do. How?

First, it has been well established that our minds don't process negatives well. If I tell you not think of a big gorilla wearing a strawberry for a hat then you'll HAVE to think of it first in order to negate/reject it. Therefore, you have already experienced the feelings you are now avoiding. Secondly, in case you secretly thought – "Well, I did experience them for a flash but then I 'contained' them and pushed them down/away because I couldn't cope with their fully intensity… don't you think that the FACT you are containing them means a) they are not strong enough to burn their way out so YOU are stronger than them b) by containing them you have put a lid of them and therefore you OWN those feelings; you are in the position of authority because – as explained before – the mental position of thinking ABOUT another thought puts you in a dominant relationship to it.

So you ARE strong enough, you HAVE stood it and you CAN decide what to do next about those feelings you have OWNERSHIP OVER.

### Notes on the 2x2

This process has a well-respected pedigree. Viktor Frankl wrote **Man's Search for Meaning** after surviving a German concentration camp. In the book he mentions a technique called 'paradoxical intent' in which you do *more* of what makes you feel uncomfortable – on purpose. Doing so, lessens its power.

The 2x2 process I'm about to describe (by Ralph Cushnir) works, in part, because you are consciously taking the mental driver's seat in allowing emotions to process through your mind and body.

Emotions were never meant to stay in our bodies but wash through like spring showers or even heavy thunderstorms. But they pass. Unless we resist them, in which case they fester and eventually go unconscious, only surfacing to sabotage our efforts at appropriate moments. Appropriate for them, that is!

### The process

Start with something that will be positive: a step you need to take to advance towards your vision and something which you are currently afraid to do:

1. What is something you need to do to advance you toward achieving your vision?

Next, identify the 'trigger': the point at which you feel the fear or other uncomfortable emotion. This is what Cushnir calls 'the flinch': the point at which your mind-body tries to feel the emotion and simultaneously tries to avoid it – the 'flinch'. This is the point at which you will be stepping INTO the flinch in order to feel it fully.

2. Identify the 'flinch' point at which you would normally resist feeling the emotion. If possible, identify what is going on in your imagination: where are you? Who are you with? What is being said and done? This is important because when the feeling fades, as it will, you'll need to revisit it and bringing these trigger activators to mind will make that happen, most of the time.

3. Weather the storm: this is the particularly tough bit yet it is utterly necessary to do for you to move forward. You must allow yourself to feel the emotion fully. I warn you: it may surprise you with the ferocity of the feelings especially if the wound is deep. The longest I have heard of the feelings-storm lasting is five minutes… the shortest I have found is about 30-45 seconds. As Winston Churchill said: 'If you are going through hell, keep going.'

But… suddenly you will awake and the mental 'air' in your head will be clear with a clarity you never have felt before.

4. Rinse and repeat. Bring to mind the 'triggers' and if there is anything left of the feeling, feel it again until it dissipates.

## Skimming

This is my term, not Cushnir's and I will explain it with a metaphor: you know when it is icy and there is a layer of frost on top of the ice. The frost, you can brush off with a hand or glove: the ice you have to apply heat and melt.

When you go hunting for triggers you may first get milder uncomfortable feelings but sense there is something else underneath them. The milder feelings are the 'frost': treat them in the manner above because once the 'forest' melts your mind may break through to a much deeper emotion.

Depending on how aware you are on your internal mind's workings (which is why I recommended image streaming) you may see-hear and feel a memory from an earlier time which is the real root cause of this. It's nothing to worry about, just process the feeling as stated above. At the most it will give you some insight into how all this started but it's only necessary as a trigger to help you wash the feelings out of your system.

### Clues on finding the feelings

Sometimes these feelings are quite subtle. If you've ever brushed part of your body and felt a lump just under the skin, one you have to go over twice to be sure that something is there; it's like this. You can't be 100% sure but you are sure enough.

## Effects whilst doing the process

I realise that telling you this is hardly 'selling' the process but whilst doing this I've burst into tears, got sudden stomach aches, and felt like vomiting. But I stayed with the process and ALWAYS felt healthier and more integrated afterwards.

Even in the moments of feeling the feelings you can still say: 'I welcome this in with kindness and care' repeatedly. You must stick with the feeling until you feel it starting to break down/subside.

### Aftermath...

Since doing this I've experienced a calm and sense of mental spaciousness that I've never experienced before. It's like those stuffed emotions were like clothes, rolled up and taking up space in my emotional head-closet.

But I'd grown so use to the restricted emotional range I could feel that it *seemed* normal. And indeed, anything you do enough, does become normal. That is why 'question normal' is one of my commandments for finding out what limitations you have accepted.

I am more at ease around my sons, even when they ignore me as teenagers are prone to do. When I notice an old feeling-thought trying to get attention I now observe it with detachment 'Oh, hello, insecurity! I'm just going to ignore you and do something else.' It works.

I did notice that for a while my behaviour got a bit more extreme. I was louder and more opinionated and less tolerant with people around me. Perhaps it was a reaction to being 'nice' for so long or perhaps, less palatably, it was the true me coming out. Whichever it was, having noticed it, I started to monitor my behaviour, not for the sake of other people but because I value treating people with respect and I wanted to do it for **me**.

I also noticed that having done this process many times my older, leftover hurt emotions rise to the surface more easily. This is a good thing because I am able to process them faster. It's like any skill: the more you practice the more easily you can use it when the time comes.

It's quite a sensation: to feel safe in your own skin, content in your own mind. There's nothing quite like it. But you have to earn it.

### After-thought

Something to realise is that anxiety, worry, depression and fears are ALL illusions regardless of how they feel. How can I say this? Simple, every single one is a *projection* of what is going to happen BUT IS NOT HAPPENING RIGHT NOW!

Therefore, to just think about them again and again is to torment yourself.

Even if someone were swinging a fist at you right now the feeling of it hitting your face would still be a future fear *until the very moment it connected* with you. I suspect this is what made Bruce Lee so fearless: that he lived in the moment of not being hit and was able to respond to every iota of movement made towards him and around him.

The moment is a quiet place.

# Fourteen: Fear of the Unknown – an illogical lie?

Fear of the unknown is probably a major reason we don't make progress. But have you ever considered that fear of the unknown is actually *fear of the new*.

This is an excellent time to mention again your *ego*: the part of you that wants to keep you safe and **only** has reference to all the things you have already done. Thus it hates and fears anything new because it thinks of it as unfamiliar.

This is the voice that tells you – 'you can't do it'; the irrational fear that stops you from speaking up and the adrenaline that keeps you moving past when you should go and ask that person out.

This neurotic lodger in your brain will always be there. Sorry. So you need to learn how to deal with him or her and act anyway. A healthy understanding that no-matter what he says, most of the time it's probably a fear based delusion is a good start.

You can build references for yourself by making a list of all the times you 'felt the fear and acted anyway' – and were successful. Firmly recalling these can help you in times of trial to realise that no matter how real it feels, it is a lie. By building a new reference for your brain you do what Einstein said was necessary and 'solve the problem from a different level to the one it was created'.

Today I had to go into a hair studio to promote a luxury hair jewelry product that I created. (www.hairmywords.com) After two years work I have to put my product out there and finally find out if people want it. This prospect does come with some fear!

I made myself walk there and reminded myself that there is no danger in the present – only in an imagined future. I walked in and asked to speak to the owner and after twenty minutes' discussion I did not leave with a sale but three leads for possible resale agents that I had not got before!

**Things are rarely completely unknown**

Our brains do love to deal in absolutes.

- I'll never be able to do that.
- You contradict me every time
- That's it. I'm done for good talking with you.

I'd like you to consider for a few moments – how often is a new situation *completely* unknown?

Our minds like to make us imagine an unknown dark void 'where be dragons' and we shirk back from the (imaginary) dark place in our minds. Yet… most situations involve people or objects externally and they all involve ideas internally.

Do you have some familiarity with how people behave? Of course you do, so what are some of the likely (I did not say *feared*) responses you could encounter?

Whether you like your answers or not does the reasonable anticipation of possible consequences ease your fear just a little bit?

When have you encountered a situation even slightly like this? What did you learn from the previous situation?

If you are convinced you have *never* experienced anything like this then who can you go to who has? What information might the internet have for you?

I was afraid for a long time of being attacked in the street (as I *was* attacked in the street when I was 15) but after buying a video called *Family Defence* I learned and mentally practiced a few things that I could do if a similar situation occurred. I also read a couple of books on learning to cope with rushes of adrenaline.

Does that mean I would survive a street attack unscathed? No. But it does mean that my confidence in acting is greater than if I had not considered *in advance* what I could do.

**What's the worst that could happen?**

It is a good idea to ask yourself: 'What's the worst that could happen?' This comes back to the whole acceptance thing: you can accept that this awful outcome might happen (yes, you can accept/acknowledge it, don't tell me you can't) and prepare yourself spiritually mentally emotionally physically for it. Reality IS your friend. It's not 'with power comes great responsibility' – acceptance/acknowledge IS storing up the power to be prepared.

I remember being alone in the house as a young boy and hearing footsteps along the downstairs hall (I was in my bedroom). The footsteps came up the stairs (because I knew which stairs creaked as I came up!) and stopped right outside my bedroom door. I KNEW the front door was locked, I hadn't heard it open and therefore the only way the person could have come in was through the insecure back porch door. I thought it was a house invasion with some guy come to rob us!

In terror, I raised my guitar above my head and ripped open the door to confront the intruder. In front of me sat *Prince*, my neighbor's Labrador-Whippet cross!

All my fear evaporated because I knew Prince, and how he behaved and I was in no danger. Yet before, I feared I was. False Evidence Appearing Real!

Thinking through what can happen in a scenario and accepting what you can and cannot influence chases away much fear, trust me. I realise some of you will be saying: 'I know what could happen, I just don't want to accept it.' My friend, let me tell you something.

There are some awful things go in this world and if they are going to try and happen to you, then they will try, whether you like it or not. It's better to accept some things will hurt or be difficult and ask yourself what you can do *anyway*. This is maturity.

Some years ago I was attacked on the street with no provocation. Three guys just came up behind me, and one circled his arm around my face and punched me in the mouth with a ring, splitting my lip.

I was in shock and didn't fight back - thank God they let me walk off bleeding but *now* I have mentally prepared a few plans of action should someone want to attack me again.

I know that being punched hurts but *accepting that* it will hurt gives me the power to go past it next time. It will still hurt, there will still be adrenaline but perhaps I will run, go for the leader or shout 'fire'.

Recently, I had to deal with a very aggressive customer at work. She made a series of unreasonable demands from my colleagues so they called me, the manager. This very fierce looking woman glared at me over her broken glasses and told loudly me that stopping her was illegal and she'd report me if I didn't give her what she wanted.

She also said that my employers were filtering her Google searches and that was illegal too....

I'm no lover of confrontation but I'd decided I was not going to give in so I just told her 'No' – like a broken record – until she gave up and stomped away. My heart was pounding and I felt a bit out of breath – all signs of adrenaline surge – but I had won – over myself!

Now she still tries to get her way but because I have 'felt the fear' and done it anyway I don't feel the anticipation of her stabbing me either. Sometimes you need to 'step out in faith'.

Look I know you think you can't deal with the emotion, the fallout etc etc. Well you can and here's the proof. You generate the emotions, don't you? And short of any genetic flaw you must have been designed to withstand and process all your emotions, right?

If you believe in God then you believe He designed you to operate successfully – and that includes successfully dealing with all your emotions. If you believe in evolution do you think 'Nature' would have designed you to 'explode' if you felt 'too much' emotion?

(By the way, when I was looking for a picture I found 'Head exploding stock images for free or for as little as $0.20' on a Google search. Amazing what's on the internet, right?)

If you can conceive it you can deal with it because you have already experienced it! What does this mean? Your mind does not process negatives well – don't think of the exploding head NOW – and has to actually experience something – however briefly – before it slaps a negation/No over it.

One little trick you can try is to give yourself permission to feel the emotion of fear/uncertainty etc. This is an old trick I learned from Professor Hall:

- What if I gave myself permission to feel X and still be 100% okay about it?
- If you keep asking this, you may feel a feeling like something settling inside you and start to feel differently about the emotion. This is permission! Now, think again about the situation that you respond in fear too

### How could this turn out for my good?

To take this attitude requires a certain amount of maturity. When something you don't like happens IF - and only IF - you are conscious enough to take a mental step back you: can ask:

What's the best that could happen? How could this turn out for my good?

Depending on how strong your mood is you may need to keep asking this until your mind responds. At first, it may say 'nothing, no good'. But if you insist, you may get an answer you like.

Recently, I lost a year's work on a website www.hairmywords.com . Everything I had done was destroyed in a server move. For about half a day I was not sure if I wanted to move ahead. But because I had trained my mind to ask the questions above I realized that I had been wanting to make some major changes to the site and had been avoiding it, because of the amount of work it would take.

Now, I had the opportunity to make those changes. So I did, and the site looks a lot more professional than it did.

Did you even think about this side of it? If not, you may have a thinking bias towards the negative which you will benefit from changing.

### How could this situation turn out for my benefit?

### Is there any benefit to this at-all?

### Another reframe on fear

Many famous actors have said that when they feel butterflies in their stomach they reframe the 'fear' as excitement – and that 'excitement' was the butterflies flying in formation!

How about thinking about the way you feel in this way: 'it is the intrigue of the new'?

After all, where does much your forthcoming success and happiness come from? If you are ambitious, then it's new things! It is human nature to attempt to actualize: to be the very best you can be.

And trust me: when you reframe you literally put a new mental frame around a thought and change its meaning. Imagine an old painting of a carved wooden door: imagine putting a frame around it decorated with brightly coloured flowers. Now, imagine putting barbed wire and dead vines around it. Changes the way you think about the content, doesn't it? That is akin to reframing, giving a new meaning to the content of a memory.

Just a thought for you: Rather than a good outcome being 'too good to be true' did you consider that a bad outcome might be 'too bad to be true'!

**Building a new response towards 'the unknown'**

If you 'fear the unknown' then try this next exercise: I apologize in advance if you find it too advanced (!) but I've included it in the hope that you'll get some benefit to it and go on to explore more material from its creator (and I don't make any money from recommending it!):

Draw a medium sized circle in the middle of a piece of paper, big enough to write in.

- What comes to mind when you think of the unknown?

Ask yourself this question ten times and write the answers down on a sheet of paper *inside the circle*

- Take a deep breath; hum happy birthday or walk up and down the garden – anything that will shake off the mood induced by answering those questions.
- Now ask yourself:
    o What if I were to feel intrigued by the unknown?
    o What if I was compelled by the curiosity of the unknown?
    o What if the fascinating new things in the 'as yet unknown' contained answers that would further the manifestation of my success?
    o What new things would I like to be able to do by calmly and mindfully handling the unknown?

- Stand up, gesture grandly, breath the feelings in deeply, act like you would if you were truly intrigued, compelled and fascinated by the prospect of growing and achieving your goals. All of this is to amplify the feelings and increase the chances of updating your existing thought. When the feelings feel as strong as they are going to get ask yourself these questions aloud?

- How do I now feel about all those thoughts of the unknown in the circle, having felt all of these amazing emotions and more?
- How does feeling these new thoughts and feelings about the unknown transform it into something more positive, hasn't it?

- Feel all of those feelings coming over, onto and into the thoughts you had about the unknown. How does having done this exercise transform those thoughts of the unknown now?
- Let the new feelings settle. Think of a situation in which you feared the unknown: imagine yourself, seeing through your own eyes and hearing what you hear and feeling what you feel dealing with that differently because

You see, outside of what you currently know – or what you have presently formulated from *what* you know, are the new perceptions, values, decisions and behaviours that could move you into the success you desire. So you NEED to do something new. You have probably heard a saying that 'the definition of insanity is doing the same thing again and again and expecting different results.'

That is also the definition of stuck. And if you are stuck you need to look at the assumptions you are making. If you have no idea which assumptions to change then just change one. Reverse it. See how your thinking is freed up. And make new decisions from there.

You see, the secret to all change in life (other than that divinely sent) is to renew your mind with new and better thoughts.

What is better? Well, I have my own views on that, some of which are shared by 2 billion other people. But it is for you to decide what will produce a healthier, more productive, moral, happy and prosperous lifestyle.

# Fifteen: Can you even see your problem, man?

One thing I stress in most of my books is the need to be able to 'look in' on what your mind is doing and see the pictures created in there.

Your mind is not a black box: it's workings can be observed and you can learn how to observe them. It's important to be able to do so because self-knowledge is a key to progress and most if not all self-knowledge is represented pictorially in your mind whether you can 'see' it or not.

Whilst doing the 'weathering the storm' exercises in chapter x I have caught glimpses of pictures and heard sounds from the original events that caused me to feel the way I feel and, as a result, I can identify, evaluate, and drain the emotion out of those events. Without that awareness it would have been much harder.

Win Wenger, genius idea generator at www.winwenger.com taught me that the mind is always showing us a stream of images in answers to the questions we pose it.

For many people these images operate outside of consciousness only breaking through the veil of consciousness at seemingly random moments.

You may have experienced this phenomenon when you lost your keys or some other item. By thinking hard about where it might be you made that question important to your mind to answer. Probably after releasing your mind in exasperation you suddenly had a feeling or a mental picture of where the item would be. You went – and you found it.

Image streaming gives you multiple benefits: you develop your ability to ask your mind questions and get useful answers; and you get flashes of insight more often even without asking as your can *see* what your mind is showing you. Remember, lies your mind tells you hide in darkness. This – is shining a light on them.

But if that is not convincing enough, then consider that the university of Minnesota did some independent research on what you are going to do, and found an increase of 1 IQ point for each hour of usage. There is some debate about how permanent that increase is, but I can attest it at least lasts for months after regular practice has stopped.

Trust me, this is well worth doing especially when you feel 'stuck' and cannot 'see' the way forward. Whilst your mind is NOT a source of infinite wisdom (have you SEEN some of the stupid decisions you made?) it does a good job of suggesting new options when you ask it properly.

**So how do you image stream?**

The basic process is very simple. You close your eyes and describe out-loud what you see to an external source (either a recording device or a person – which is better). Whether you only start by seeing the vaguest clouds or dots of light or you see soaring mountains, it does not matter. You describe it using ONLY sensory words: things you can see-hear-feel-smell-touch. No judgements allowed, so no "I see a beautiful rose" rather "I see a red rose with flecks of white near the central stalk. I smell its perfume, and my fingers feel its silky leaves."

As you keep describing do not stop, always reach for the most accurate descriptions you can and you will find the image changes, mutates into something different. Keep describing out loud.

There's a lot of different ways to do this so I have provided a link to a free book: Two Guaranteed Ways to Profoundly Increase your Intelligence:

http://www.winwenger.com/ebooks/guaran4.htm

**and other helpful information here:**

http://www.winwenger.com/imstream.htm

Win challenges people to do the TEN/TEN test. Do this for ten minutes a day for ten days and see if your life does not start to change profoundly. If not, do something else.

# Sixteen: Thinking through the influence of childhood memories and frames of reference

I realize some of you, maybe most of you will not be ready to read this. But more and more I conclude that our childhood memories and conclusions about life don't *need* to have as much effect as we let them do. Notice I did not say they don't have an effect. They do. Until we come to terms with and change them.

'Oh', you may say, - 'you haven't been through what I have been through!' Well, I don't think comparing scars is useful because there is always someone worse off than me or you and… out of those people there are examples of ones that have risen above their experiences: Helen Keller comes to mind – born blind and deaf and mute who, with the help of an incredible teacher, rose to international fame and to inspire millions.

But to give you an idea of what I have overcome – for the sake of you knowing this advice comes from a place of authenticity:

My mother was institutionalized soon after I was born; and parented by overly authoritarian parents she went on to become what I think of us as an undiagnosed schizophrenic terror.

I lived in an atmosphere of constant fear: I never knew when she would blow up and then be as nice as you would want. She was overly controlling; lacked personal boundaries and would have fits of rage that could be so strong she would try and break my bedroom door down if I resisted her. Do you know what that was like? Watching the plaster around your bedroom door crack as an enraged mother threw herself against it trying to break it down so she could get her out of control hands on me? I was beaten with a vacuum pipe, lifted up by the throat, and I expect I have forgotten some of the other stuff. At school I was bullied to the point of a nervous breakdown by a gang of kids in my year; and gangs roamed the streets in East London where I lived. Basically, life was a fear-fest inside and outside of the house.

But here's the conclusion I have come to…

You secretly trust your own memories MORE – probably because they are YOURS (and nobody tells the Truth like you!) and possibly because you have confused familiarity with Truthfulness. Specifically, you believe that because you've had a way of thinking and feeling for a long time – and in a strange way you are comfortable and familiar with it – therefore it MUST be true.

Rubbish.

In fact, the conclusions you made, the beliefs you developed as a child should be the LEAST trustworthy of all! As an adult now you have so much more experience and information about life to draw upon. The conclusions you drew as a kid were narrow, based on limited data and all kinds of thinking errors. You didn't know what to think because you didn't KNOW what there was to think. Most kids blame themselves for their parent's breakup, right? Why? Because kids lack data and time and perspective. Not because they are all correct!

You should be more willing to doubt and question the conclusions you made about life, the universe and everything as a kid SIMPLY BECAUSE YOU WERE A DUMB KID! I really am not being nasty – this is a freeing truth.

If there is a high chance you could have been wrong then this is an excellent chance for you to revise any conclusions you made! Unless you believe the rubbish that our personalities are formed by age eight? I am not doubting the influence of genetics and hormones but I am asking you if you really think that what happened to you as a kid should be deterministic. What studies was that based on anyway? Most neuroscientists these days understand that the brain has great plasticity meaning it can be reshaped right up to the day you die!

Maybe basic personality is formed by age 8 – but not permanently!

Reflecting on the above means you can conclude that what you grew up believing *doesn't have to be true!*

# About me (it may be useful to know!)

I've been using personal development for about twenty years and writing about it for five. I've read hundreds of books, attended courses, and done more personal change-work that I can remember.

I've coached others professionally and had coaching and therapy myself. Some of it has helped but in the end, the deepest wounds were still there.

Did I mention I was emotionally and physically abused as a child? That I lived in terror of my mother who has now died but probably was highly mentally ill?

Did I mention that she was prone to rage and anger like flash floods? That she squashed any sign of individualism in me?

The result of this was that I spent most of my teenage and young adult life dealing with self-loathing and denial of that self-loathing. I tried to numb my deep seated beliefs about myself with success – and addictions when my 'personal truth' started peeping through the cracks.

I didn't medicate with drugs: my drugs were the thirst for knowledge plus a healthy dose of junk food, sex, and entertainment. Anything to stop me having to sit quietly with myself and listen to those inner voices.

During those times I had an interesting life so far and I've done some interesting things (well, I think so!)

- I've been as far around the world as South America one way and New Zealand the other. I nearly broke my leg falling off a high pavement in the dark in a crime ridden area of Ota Hu Hu, Auckland, and had to drag myself back to the hotel with locals refusing to stop in case I was a set-up for a car-jacking.
- I've survived a divorce, church break-up, job-loss, home loss and cat-loss all in the period of a year. I nearly ended up killing myself over that only for it to form a major part of my journey to writing this book.
- I've written ten books (this is the eleventh) and had one of them sell perhaps a thousand copies so far. The other I've perhaps sold thirty of each! This is the slow path to success!
- I invented customisable hair jewellery and got the design registered by the British Government. You can take a look at www.hairmywords.com

- I fought the British Government in court twice to get my wife and her children over from South America. I acted as our own lawyer, and we won. Did I say twice? I'm proud of that.
- I've worked for the top-selling weekly women's magazine in Britain, landing a job there in two weeks that took other journalists five years to earn. I also worked in Harrods selling over-priced doorknobs to rich people serving guys with names like Mr B'stard. Really.
- Set up and run a professional coaching business for four years coaching ministers, health care professionals and housewives.
- Preached sermons and given talks in London colleges on meaning and the mind.
- Been remarried nine years, blissfully happy. Five-year-old daughter between us and five other children ranging in colours from white through to brown. Love them all.

I guess at first glance it would seem like my life has been a mad scramble for success overcoming obstacles on the way: sometimes falling down, sometimes rising up. Probably not that different to a lot of other people: maybe even you.

But perhaps the more interesting reason is I now know *why* I did all of this. I'll come to that because it will be essential for you to know. Because the reason I have strived to overcome and succeed is the same reason you are doing the same. You may not like my answer; but it's the most accurate one I've found and I'm at peace with it.

*We are born with a deep desire to actualize: to be the best possible version of ourselves we can be. We let life derail us from actualizing and spend a lifetime either striving for it or medicating ourselves because we are stuck/ignorant of it.*

That's the bit you probably like and agree with.

I believe the truest image of human-kind's fully developed potential is Jesus Christ. He is what every man and women is intended to look like. That doesn't mean I think every person needs to become a minister in a church but it does mean that I think you are missing something if you don't strive to know God and His Son.

I said you might not like it which is why I left it till last. Not because I am ashamed but because so many people (not you of course) have ignorant closed and reactive minds when it comes to anything spiritual. They, of course, are the worst fundamentalists – the ones that cannot possibly conceive they could be wrong because everyone else is.

I chose to become a Christian at 23 – at first mostly out of desperation. Maybe God could heal me and rid me of this pain. And over the years – He has – not in the way I wanted which was a flash-bang-I'm-cured kind of way but rather in an ever evolving set of insights which have helped me heal and given me wisdom which I can share with you. And the mad thirst for knowledge became a source of useful help techniques and understandings many of which you're going to read.

Once the pain started clearing away I was able to think more clearly about what I desired to do with my life. I discovered I am a multipotentiate – someone with multiple interests and talents.

I discovered that it's okay to not have one single life purpose (check out www.puttylike.com for more details) and I could contribute in several areas of life.

For me, and perhaps for you, the ultimate goal for myself always was and is freedom of self-expression, what you might call 'authenticity': I want to present 'myself' to the world without shame or excuse.

You might say simply: 'I want to be me.'

So I adjusted my approach and set out to find out how to access and overcome those wounds. What I found, I think had always known.

We are so desperate for truth we will cling onto our own thoughts and swear they are true *simply because they are ours*. We would rather be comfortable in misery than uncomfortable and wrong so we could open up and change!

I truly believe we are made for a higher purpose than just existing. We are made for God and not to be our own God. We have a God who loves us, who sent His Son to save us from ourselves and who works mysteriously in our lives.

If you are in the least bit curious, you can contact me. Or go to a church. I don't have all the answers. I don't know exactly why there is so much evil in the world although I have some thoughts.

I don't understand exactly why there are 30,000 different interpretations of Christianity or why the Bible has dozens of different translations. I struggle in my faith.

But I believe in Jesus the Christ. Read about Him. Think it over. Pray. There is no-one like Him nor will there ever be. He is Lord.

Let Him be yours.

34421341R00048

Printed in Great Britain
by Amazon